THE JESUS AGENDA

THE JESUS AGENDA

Becoming An Agent of Redemption

Albert L. Reyes, DMin, PhD

BelieversPress

THE JESUS AGENDA

ISBN: 978-0-578-16292-8

Buckner International
700 N. Pearl Street, Suite 1200 (12th floor)
Dallas, TX 75201

Printed in the United States of America

BelieversPress

To the exceptional leaders and staff of Buckner International who selflessly serve everyday as agents of redemption, shining hope into the lives of vulnerable children, orphans, seniors and their families.

CONTENTS

INTRODUCTION

Why Write This Book?

The Spirit of the Lord is on me, because he has anointed me to preach good news to the poor. He has sent me to proclaim freedom for the prisoners and recovery of sight for the blind, to release the oppressed, to proclaim the year of the Lord's favor.

LUKE 4:18-19

I chose to write this book because I wanted to tell my story of redemption and encourage followers of Jesus to become agents of redemption. Weeks and months before I addressed the members of the Executive Board of the Baptist General Convention of Texas (BGCT) for the first time in January of 2005, I searched the Bible for a theme, a message, a point of reference that would focus our work and efforts during the year I would serve as president of the two million-member convention of Texas Baptist Christians. I settled on a passage from the Gospel of Luke describing the first sermon of Jesus at the synagogue in Nazareth. I was drawn by the vision Jesus outlined in his first sermon. It appeared to be an agenda for his ministry on earth so I called it "The Jesus Agenda." I challenged my fellow Texans, comprised of 5,500 churches and 23 institutions (universities, hospital systems, human welfare agencies, and other affiliated ministries), to implement "The Jesus Agenda" of preaching good news to the poor, proclaiming freedom for the prisoners, recovering sight for the blind, releasing the oppressed, and proclaiming the year of the Lord's favor for everyone in our circle of influence. I was glad to find this passage but did not expect the passage to find me.

At the time I was president of the BGCT, I was also serving as president of Baptist University of the Américas (BUA)[1], a theological university in San Antonio, Texas, founded originally as the Mexican Baptist Bible Institute in 1947. Prior to serving at BUA, I was privileged to serve as pastor of three Texas churches, in Dallas and El Paso. My story of redemption and my ministry experiences were on course to intersect with the vision of Jesus in his ministry agenda. The message of "The Jesus Agenda" slowly became a part of my thinking across the ministry assignments the Lord led me to and has since then been a compass for my ministry.

My first pastoral assignment was Home Gardens Baptist Church, which later became Iglesia Bautista Alfa (Alfa Baptist Church), located in an economically depressed area of southeast Dallas. My second pastoral assignment was across from Love Field Airport at North Temple Baptist Church in Dallas, again, in a transitional and economically depressed area. My third pastoral assignment led my wife Belinda and me to El Paso, Texas where we started Pueblo Nuevo Community Church in a middle class neighborhood. Almost 20 years later, the church relocated to Clint, Texas (east of El Paso), an economically challenged area. Looking back over my pastoral ministry, the Lord sent me to places where I would have ample opportunity to preach good news to the poor, to help set captives free, to help people find healing, to reverse situations of oppression, and to introduce the hope of the Lord's favor for their lives.

My ministry focus at BUA was no different. I was to lead the school to obtain a Certificate of Authority to grant Bachelor of Arts degrees from the Texas Higher Education Coordinating Board and to achieve accredited membership with the Association of Biblical Higher Education. By 2006 these two milestones were reached in record time and in the spirit of "The Jesus Agenda" by changing the future of BUA, its students, staff, and faculty forever. The certification and accreditation conferred on BUA made it possible for ministry students, primarily of Hispanic cultural background, with limited access to higher education to earn an accredited Bachelor of Arts degree at BUA and to build a bridge to graduate studies for those who would otherwise not have the opportunity to obtain a graduate theological degree.[2] Today, many of those students have earned master of art degrees, enrolled in doctoral programs, and have earned terminal graduate theological degrees resulting in a new generation of cross-cultural ministry leaders from the Hispanic faith community serving in churches and ministries across the nation and world. The growing Hispanic population across the United States seemed to demand the preparation of many more academically qualified leaders with degrees and diplomas. My work at BUA was fueled by an ethical mission to set a new trajectory for BUA and its students, to do justice by creating access to higher education for emerging Hispanic leaders, and to develop a whole new paradigm for Hispanic theological education. I was on a redemptive mission that fit hand and glove with "The Jesus Agenda."

Today, I serve as President and CEO of Buckner International based in Dallas, Texas, a global multi-service ministry focused on making life better for vulnerable children, orphans, seniors and their families through redemptive transformation. Buckner serves seniors through retirement campuses and impacts the lives of thousands of vulnerable children, orphans, and families in the United States and across the globe in multiple countries. My vision for Buckner is to maximize resources and leadership to serve children, seniors, and their families locally and globally. Buckner reaches its clients through and beyond social services to serve many of the 200 million orphans around the world and thousands of children in the United States to help them develop their redemptive potential. At Buckner, I am on a redemptive mission in the spirit of "The Jesus Agenda." The passage I found in Luke 4 has found me over and over again.

After my year as president of Texas Baptists, I continued to think about the agenda of Jesus and found that it began to shape my thinking about what Jesus intended when he quoted from the prophet Isaiah. I began to wonder how the church that Jesus died for reflected the vision of his first sermon. Several questions began to fill my mind and heart. What would it mean in the 21st century to preach good news to the poor? What would good news for the poor look like? What would it mean for Buckner International and for me personally to serve the prisoner, the blind, the oppressed, and to announce the Lord's favor? What does it mean today for you and for me? What does that first sermon preached in the synagogue by Jesus have to do with our lives, our families, our churches, our ministries, and the Kingdom of God? My answers to these questions emerge from my own story of redemption.

MY STORY OF REDEMPTION

My story of redemption began in the early 1930s on a farm near Snyder, Texas. My paternal grandparents, José Maria Reyes and Francisca Rodriguez Reyes carved out a living with their nine children by picking cotton in the fields of West Texas as migrant workers. My father recounts the story of picking cotton all day long with the hopes of filling a 100-pound burlap sack of cotton for seventy-five cents pay and living off of beans and tortillas three times a day. This is the closest understanding I know of my family ever being poor. During one of those harvest seasons, a missionary/church planter by the name of Rev. Edward P. González gathered migrant workers and their families to hold evangelistic services. It was in those services that my paternal grandmother, Francisca Rodriguez Reyes, opened her heart to the good news of the gospel of salvation. She prayed to receive Jesus Christ as her savior and was baptized there in the watering hole used for the cows and horses on the farm. My grandfather also prayed to receive Christ as his savior sometime later. Then one by one, each of my uncles and aunts came to saving faith in Jesus. My grandfather, a first-generation native Texan and an orphaned child, was now grafted into the family of faith.[3] The Reyes family settled in Corpus Christi, Texas and began attending Primera Iglesia Bautista Mexicana, the First Mexican Baptist Church of Corpus Christi. My father's pastor and discipler at Primera was Dr. Ignacio E. González, who graduated with his classmate and friend, President Lyndon B. Johnson at Texas State University (formerly Southwest Texas State University), in San Marcos, Texas.[4]

My father, Agustín Reyes, later married Gloria Garcia of Corpus Christi, and they began attending Primera. My mother was raised in the Roman Catholic faith tradition and began attending Primera with my father. By the time I was born, my mother prayed to receive Christ as her savior, was baptized, and became a member of Primera. After moving to Southern California in the 1960s, we became members of Memorial Baptist Church where Rev. Leonard Roten and later, Rev. Bill Thornton were our pastors. I remember the day I came home from church and asked my mother how I could know my sins were forgiven and how I might have eternal life. She shared her faith and showed me God's plan for my salvation. I opened my heart to Jesus and my parents led me in a prayer to receive Christ as my savior at home. The next Sunday, I shared my new faith with Pastor Thornton and the church.

About a year later I was baptized into the fellowship of Memorial Baptist Church of Rialto, California.

My family returned to Corpus Christi in the early 1970s and we became members of my father's home church at Primera Corpus. Dr. Rudy Hernández was pastor when we first arrived at Primera. His evangelistic zeal shaped my thinking about my responsibility to share the good news of Jesus with friends and family. He was followed by Dr. Rudy Sánchez as pastor at Primera. At the age of 15, I answered a call to vocational ministry under Dr. Sánchez's ministry. He immediately put me to work and asked me to lead the children's service on Sunday mornings. By the time I was 16, he invited me to preach my first sermon at Primera. I remember Dr. Sánchez's heart and passion for the entire community, beyond the congregation he served. He was focused on developing relationships with leaders of other faiths as well as business and political leaders. He saw himself as their pastor, too. After I left Corpus Christi for college and seminary, I later came to appreciate Dr. Sánchez's passion for the least of these, the alienated, the marginalized, the oppressed, the orphan, and the widow. He seemed to always be concerned with the neglected, the under-privileged, and the economically challenged. I learned later that he was an orphaned as child. His passion for the poor and his calling to the community-at-large continues to shape my thinking and ministry today. I can see the story of redemption written all over my past, my calling, my journey in ministry, my mentors, pastors, and coaches, and my responsibility today as the leader of a vast ministry. Unlike many of his generation, Dr. Sánchez saw the connection between evangelism and social ministry.

My own educational experience at Angelo State University, Southwestern Seminary, and Andrews University provided a seamless mosaic of God's redemptive activity in my life and development as a servant. Experiences in business, ministry, higher education administration, and missions all reflect God's weaving and shaping of my life into his redemptive plan for me and those in my circle of influence.[5] I live with the conviction that I was blessed to bless others, saved to share with others, and redeemed for a purpose in God's story of redemption. My story is part of God's story of redemption. I have become an agent of redemption; called into service by Jesus my Redeemer!

WHO IS THIS BOOK WRITTEN FOR?

The greatest resource for God's redemptive mission on earth are followers of Jesus who faithfully participate in a local congregation, house church, home church, or small group week after week, yet are under-utilized and under-challenged for their own God-given call to redemptive work. Honestly, my first audience is the follower of Jesus who does not have an official leadership role or title in vocational ministry. I am writing to business leaders, lawyers, educators, engineers, teachers, professors, skilled-workers, homemakers, accountants, health professionals, middle and high school students, college students, graduate students, and service workers who long to make a difference and want to be on personal mission with God in the world. You have great potential as agents of redemption with the calling, the gifting, the experience, and resources needed to make a difference in redemptive history.

The second audience I am writing to includes seminary students, Bible college students, theological faculty and administrators, leaders in Christian higher education, pastoral leaders, missionaries, and vocational ministers. You are the key to developing and unleashing agents of redemption in your ministry and circles of influence. I pray as I write that you will receive my message with grace and openness. You are in a strategic role to advance the shift of missions engagement from the pulpit to the pew, from the ordained to the ordinary. We have unprecedented opportunities to send out scores of Jesus followers every week, every semester, every year to get engaged with God's redemptive mission locally and globally. Many of you are already making redemptive history. May the Lord multiply your tribe.

The third audience I am addressing includes ministry leaders, mission leaders and strategists, mission executives, agency executives, and denominational leaders. I am hopeful that we will find our way toward collaboration for the sake of the Redeemer's Kingdom. Self-preservation and self-interest that precludes Kingdom collaboration in redemptive work fails to activate the imagination of the Holy Spirit or the people he guides on a daily basis. We have unprecedented opportunities to make a global difference through our leadership if we dare collaborate. We live in a wired world, which make connections not only possible, but essential to the Kingdom of Christ. Without collaboration, we settle for small dreams rather than God-sized work. Jesus never intended for us to live or serve in isolation. I believe the post-denominational era we live in demands that we find common, biblical grounds to work together to build the Kingdom of Christ rather than our own kingdoms. It is incumbent upon you, as leaders of ministries and executives to look to one another for our common purpose and vision for the Kingdom impact.

WHAT IS MY APPROACH?

Chapter One defines what I mean by "redemption" from a biblical and theological perspective. Chapters Two and Three survey what the Old Testament and New Testaments say about redemption and the Redeemer. Chapter Four explores what an agent of redemption is, and Chapter Five looks at what it means to do redemption globally followed by what redemptive work looks like locally in Chapter Six. Chapter Seven shares my vision for collaborative redemption and what it would take to make the nations glad. I have started this book with a brief summary of my own story of redemption and will share additional stories of redemption as you read through these chapters. While the title of this book is "The Jesus Agenda" don't miss the subtitle - "Becoming an Agent of Redemption." It is my hope and prayer that something in this book would ignite a passion in you to shine hope through your life, your work, your ministry, your family, in your community, and around the world as an agent of redemption.

DISCUSSION QUESTIONS

1. After reading Luke 4:18-19, how does The Jesus Agenda intersect with your life, your family, your small group, your church, and your community?

2. How would your profession or vocational skills benefit the poor, those in prison, the physically challenged, and those who are oppressed in your community?

3. What is your story of redemption?

4. What do you think your role might be in serving the least of these, the 151 million orphans in the world today?

ONE:

What Do I Mean by Redemption?

For he has rescued us from the dominion of darkness and brought us into the kingdom of the Son he loves, in whom we have redemption, the forgiveness of sins.

COLOSSIANS 1:13-14

"I HAVE NEVER, NEVER KNOWN PEACE LIKE THIS BEFORE."

Dear Buckner leaders,

> "I started to remember the way it used to be living with their dad back then. Fighting every night, crying, chain smoking, stress, I was suicidal, out of control, no coping skills, a nervous wreck with no hope, all I did was yell and scream and I had very few happy moments, never had true joy before. You have to understand that I have never, never known peace like this before."

As I was preparing a presentation for the annual staff retreat of

Buckner International leaders, an email came across my screen with a letter from the first resident of a program we were beginning in a new city. I was preparing my vision speech for the coming year and knew as soon as I read the letter that I had to share Wendi's story. Wendi Hay and her three girls had recently settled into her new home and she paused in the midst of an incredibly hectic time in her life to write a thank-you note. Listen to her story of redemption:

> "I just finished up my homework for the night and I wanted to write you before I went to bed. The girls and I finished homework and chores a little early tonight so we went for a swim in the pool before bed and it was so much fun! Shauna swims like a fish now! We have taken over a thousand pictures since we have been here! I let them sleep in my bed tonight and I watched them all fall asleep peacefully. I was struck by this sense of peace. I am really growing more responsible everyday and I am finally learning to manage my life again. More importantly, I am slowly learning to manage myself. That's a big one!!! Everything is so perfect and even my college education and my career goal, business management, is so closely tied into my own personal development. Everything that I am being taught is working so well and so complete together.
>
> "I have to say thank you again for allowing me to be your first client. I don't know who contributes to your program, but I wish I could tell them what they have done for me and my children. This whole experience has really formed the faith of my

> children at a very young age. Their foundation is certainly being built on a solid and true Rock! Their faith in God will be unshakable as they mature and grow. I am finally getting over the shock of all these blessings and finally realizing and seeing the reality of all the miracles that are occurring in my life through the hand of God which has worked through His servants.
>
> "There are no limits to what my children can and will accomplish in this world with this type of upbringing. My understanding of giving has also transformed tremendously as well. I do know that once I have reached financial success, I am a guaranteed certified future philanthropist!
>
> "Our family would never have survived if it wasn't for organizations like Buckner partnering with other non-profits to create a more holistic service for families in trouble. God bless and thank you for saying yes to God!"

Left to ourselves, we tend to find our own way to life without meaning, no sense of direction, life without hope, maybe even the belief that suicide is the best answer, and very few happy moments in between. We allow what was intended to harm us, to kill us, to kill joy, happiness, a sense of meaning, direction, and purpose because, in and of ourselves, we are powerless to fix our lives, to finding meaning, and purpose. If you are like me, I have needed my life and the lives of those around me to be fixed. I have needed healing from the bumps and bruises of life. I have faced devastation, failure, depression, and have been on the edge of no hope. I have a craving for meaning and purpose. I want to know how, why, and if my life matters. I want to know if there is a reason why I was put on the planet beyond survival and success. I think redemption has something to do with the answer I seek. I think Jesus, the Redeemer of our lives, holds the answer.

Wendi and many families like hers participate in a program Buckner International developed in the mid-1990s called Family Place designed to keep children where they belong — with mom, rather than pulling the family apart by removing children from the home. It is a ministry where families are healed, safety and security are provided, families are re-built, and futures are reconstructed. Counseling, spiritual development, and educational opportunities are provided for women and children who find themselves in difficult situations. In short, families are redeemed not only in their personal faith but their whole lives are brought into a zone of living where Jesus guides, provides, and helps them make sense out of life. Every difficult experience from the past is turned into something good through this program. The testimonies of the families who participate in this ministry arrive at the same glad destination in a thousand unique ways. What could have been forever devastating and harmful is turned into something good, something redeemed.

Redemption is God's movement in history to rescue individuals from the dominion of darkness into the realm of the Kingdom of Jesus, his Son. Our redemption speaks primarily to our need for forgiveness and restoration through a right relationship with God, but our redemption also has the potential to radically transform everything about us — our purpose, our meaning, our future, our families, our communities, and our world.

REDEMPTION FROM A PRISON HOUSE

If there was ever a person who needed redeeming in the history of humanity, it would be a man by the name of Saul. Saul was a first century rabbi, teacher, expert in the Jewish law, a religious fanatic. He was a religious terrorist with authorization to hunt, persecute, arrest, and destroy a new religious sect focused on Jesus of Nazareth as their leader. Saul apprehended Christians and put them to death for their departure from the Jewish faith to which Saul pledged allegiance. On one of Saul's journeys on the road to Damascus in modern Syria, he was blinded by a very bright light as recorded by Dr. Luke in Acts of the Apostles, chapter 9. Saul fell from his horse to the ground, blinded by the light and heard a voice from heaven saying, "Saul, Saul, why do you persecute me?" "Who are you Lord?" Saul asked. The voice answered "I am Jesus whom you are persecuting, now get up and go into the city and you will be told what to do."

Saul went into Damascus and met with a man by the name of Ananias who served him and helped him regain his strength. The Lord Jesus also spoke to Ananias in a vision instructing him to assist Saul and help to restore his sight. Ananias said to Saul, "the Lord Jesus, who appeared to you on the road as you were coming here, has sent me so that you may see again and be filled with the Holy Spirit. Scales immediately fell off of Saul's eyes and he could see again. Saul got up and was immediately baptized, ate some food and regained his strength. Soon after this experience Saul, whose name was changed to Paul, began preaching in the synagogues that Jesus is the son of God.

Paul was called and commissioned by the Lord Jesus Christ to be his apostle to the Gentiles. Over the span of the rest of his life Paul would preach, make disciples for Jesus, and start churches throughout the Middle East and Southern Europe and then write letters back to those churches to strengthen and encourage them.

One such letter was written while Paul was in Rome in prison. He wrote a letter to the Christians who were part of a house church in Colossae, a city about 100 miles east of Ephesus. While Paul had not met the Christians in that church and had not visited Colossae, he sent

Epaphras there to get the church started. During their pagan days, the Colossian Christians expressed their hostility to God by doing evil deeds but after they placed their faith in Christ, they began living lives worthy of the name of Jesus. They previously lived under the influence of spirit principalities and powers, evil forces, which kept the Colossians in the grip of evil with devastating effects. As Gentiles, they previously lived without God and without hope but now they were kept in Christ and full of hope of a better life. Paul wrote to correct philosophies, false notions, and human traditions that were contrary to what they learned in their new faith in Christ. Paul raised the triad of love, faith, and hope as a description of their new life in Christ, and he taught that beyond forgiveness of sin and the break from a life dominated by sin that they had been redeemed and transferred into living in the light rather than darkness into the kingdom of Jesus.

From a prison house to a church house, Paul writes about redemption. In an effort to dig deeper into the meaning of redemption, I will examine portions of this letter written by Paul to the Colossians. Since English was not the international language of Paul's day, I will take a look at Koine Greek, the language of the New Testament and the language spoken by people of the Roman empire, including Colossae, in the first century.

REDEMPTION AS RESCUE FROM THE DOMINION OF DARKNESS

Jesus is the author, the initiator, the architect of redemption. It is his movement in the world, in history, and in our lives to rescue us from the dominion of darkness. To be redeemed is to be rescued out from (*ek*) the power (*exousias*) of the kingdom of darkness (*skotous*) in which we were held as slaves.[1] The Apostle Paul, in his letter to the church in Colossae, says we were rescued out of the grip of darkness. *Exousias* is a sphere of power and authority, especially in the spiritual sense. *Sko-*

tous used with *exousias* is a sphere of darkness, of future punishment, and the power of the underworld.[2] The idea here is that of "dragging a person out of battle or the jaws of danger."[3] This is the domain of Satan and his demons, a spirit world that is not always visible but whose atmosphere and impact is unmistakable to everyone who has ever been in its grip.

When Wendy wrote her thank you note and described how she spent her time fighting, stressed out, out of control, suicidal, and a nervous wreck with very few moments of happiness, I am reminded of Paul's teaching about the dominion of darkness. In Ephesians 6:12 he says "For our struggle is not against flesh and blood, but against the rulers, against the authorities, against the powers of this dark world and against the spiritual forces of evil in the heavenly realms." Paul acknowledged the reality and existence of an evil sphere of influence. Even though we cannot often see this world, we can see the affects of evil forces and their influence on people in the visible world. I am convinced the dominion of darkness exists, and I have seen its negative impact on the lives of people enslaved and impacted by this lifestyle. Wendy lived in this space day after day, under this dominion, until she came to faith in Christ.

The dominion of darkness is ruled by Satan, the deceiver. Speaking to religious leaders, John the apostle quotes Jesus in John 8:44 saying, "You belong to your father, the devil, and you want to carry out your father's desire. He was a murderer from the beginning, not holding to the truth, for there is no truth in him. When he lies, he speaks his native language, for he is a liar and the father of lies."

Satan is also contrasted with Jesus as one who takes life rather than giving life. In John 10:10, Jesus says, "The thief comes only to steal, kill, and destroy; I have come that they might have life, and have it to the full." In essence, the mission of Satan and the dominion of darkness are to steal, kill, and destroy everything that God intended for your life. The dominion of darkness is not satisfied until God's blessings are stolen, the abundant life intended for you is killed, and all the good and perfect gifts God wants for you are destroyed.

When Jesus comes to rescue us from the dominion of darkness, our sins are forgiven and we are eternally free from spiritual slavery to this sphere of spiritual authority; we are free to believe and live according to the truth rather than a lie. What was stolen is restored. What was killed is resurrected back to life. What was destroyed is remade through our relationship with our Redeemer, Jesus Christ.

REDEMPTION AS A TRANSITION TO THE KINGDOM OF JESUS

Colossians 1:13 says "...and (God) brought us into the kingdom of the Son he loves..." In the common Greek language of Paul's readers, the word for "brought" is *metestesen*, meaning to remove, transplant into, to bring to a different point of view, or to cause someone to change his/her position.[4] One commentator uses the word "translated" to denote the "transplanting of races and the settlement of them in a new home; a resettlement of the captives in the new kingdom of Christ."[5] Rather than living under the dominion of darkness, Jesus relocates us into another realm of existence, the kingdom of light, the kingdom of the Son God loves. When Wendy moved into the Buckner program she underwent a resettlement of sorts. She came onto the Buckner campus and was physically resettled into a new living zone. More importantly, she also came into a different spiritual zone of encouragement and support when she arrived at Buckner.

When Jesus taught his disciples how to pray in Matthew 6:9 he gave them three priorities to focus on in prayer: God's name, God's Kingdom, and God's will on earth as it is in heaven. The Kingdom of God was foremost in his teaching and in his ministry. Jesus taught that the Kingdom of God is near (Matthew 3:2) and he started many of his parables with this introductory phrase: "The Kingdom of God is like…" to illustrate the reality of the Kingdom in terms his hearers could grasp. Arthur Glasser categorized the parables of Jesus into growth, banquet, stewardship, and seeking themes. The growth parables teach that the Kingdom of God, his sovereign and creative activity in history and throughout the world is constantly advancing; the banquet parables teach that kingdom service requires collaboration with Jesus in holiness and social responsibility by prophetic words and loving deeds; the stewardship parables teach personal responsibility and accountability of the good news of the kingdom; and the seeking parables teach the value and worth of the kingdom over material possessions.[6] The Kingdom of God was not only foremost in the teachings of Jesus but also the core of his first sermon in Luke 4:14-30. Wendy's story is a growth parable. Her story magnifies the truth that God is sovereign in her life creatively working through her and her children for the future of the Kingdom.

Jesus also taught that seeking the Kingdom of God should be our first priority over everything else. In Matthew 6:33, Jesus said "But seek first the kingdom and his righteousness, and all these things will be given to you as well." Jesus teaches that if we seek his kingdom and God's righteousness, everything else we need will be given to us. This kingdom of the Son God was such a priority to God that he sent his only Son to earth to establish this kingdom on earth as it is in heaven. The kingdom must also be a priority to those who call Jesus their Redeemer, their King.

The kingdom of the Son God loves is, according to Tullian Tchividjian,[7] a kingdom where God's appointed king, Jesus, is presently reigning in and through the lives of his people, accomplishing his will "on earth as it is in heaven." This implies that the values of the Kingdom of Jesus take root in our hearts and minds as well as our actions. Kingdom people live differently in every area of life as they begin to seek the values of the kingdom as their highest priority. Values of justice, integrity, truth, honesty, wholeness, healing, joy, peace, patience, kindness, goodness, meekness, and self-control are all markers of this kingdom. This is the point of view that we have been resettled to, from the dominion of darkness by the work and life of Jesus, our Redeemer. This is our new way of life and our new way of viewing the world. This new life is made possible by the sacrifice of Jesus and the redemption of our lives. Or to say it another way, kingdom people are redeemed citizens. We have been rescued from the dominion of darkness and purchased by the blood of Christ and restored to a right relationship with God. We who have been rescued and redeemed are now agents of the very redemption that bought us.

Wendy was resettled into a new realm of existence when she came to Buckner. Once her life began to change and she began to see her life change through a new way of thinking, a new sense of self-worth, and a new way of living, she saw that her life was being redeemed. It was at that point that she began to become an agent of redemption for the lives of her children. Everything about their lives changed from that point forward.

It is through redemption that we are reconciled to God and brought into his kingdom. The very word "atonement" means "at one with God." Our reconciliation with God through redemption is being made right with God by God. It is his work of grace and our unmerited favor. Paul said in Colossians that through Jesus Christ, God reconciled all things to himself, having made peace through the blood of his cross." Nowhere in scripture is God reconciled to us. Rather, God reconciles us to himself. He does the work and then he gives the work of reconciliation as his ambassadors, his agents of redemption and reconciliation. Second Corinthians 5:18-20 tells us that God reconciled us to himself through Christ and "gave us the ministry of reconciliation, namely, that God was in Christ reconciling the world to himself." Therefore, "we are ambassadors for Christ."

REDEMPTION AS FORGIVENESS OF OUR SINS

The transformation from the dominion of darkness to the kingdom of light, the Kingdom of Jesus, brings with it the forgiveness of sins. Paul says to the Colossians (Colossians 1:14) that we have been resettled to the kingdom of the Son God loves "in whom we have redemption, the forgiveness of sins." True redemption of our lives starts with the opportunity to be forgiven for our sins, to receive the grace that God has for us through the sacrifice of Jesus on the cross.

The word in the Greek language of Paul's day for redemption in this passage is *apolutrosis*, meaning a "releasing, on payment of a ransom… indicating both the liberation from the guilt and doom of sin and the introduction into a life of liberty and newness."[8] The payment for our sins was the ransom Jesus paid with his own life (Mark 10:45; Matthew 20:28; and John 3:16) that provides release for us from the slavery and bondage to sin and the dominion of darkness into the kingdom of his son. The ransom is the "purchase-money in freeing slaves."[9] This makes all things new for every person related to Jesus through faith. In Christ, we are no longer slaves to the dominion of sin but we are free to live a life fully redeemed for God's purpose and for his Kingdom. Through the blood of Jesus Christ, God made complete payment to buy us out of the slavery to sin and release us from the domain of darkness, transferring us to his kingdom.

Everything that Satan intended for evil, God reverses for good through redemption. This cosmic transaction not only determines the eternal destiny of our soul but the reality of the Kingdom of God in our lives on earth. In redemption, our lives, our purpose, our families, our neighborhood, our community, and our circle of influence come into the range of potential transformation by the presence of God's kingdom. You have the opportunity to have your life redeemed in this way by receiving God's gift of redemption, turning away from sin, and living in the freedom of his love for you. We have the opportunity to live as a brand new people in Christ. The Apostle Paul says it this way: "Therefore, if anyone is in Christ, he is a new creation; the old has gone, the new has come!" (2 Corinthians 5:17).

Margarita Acosta's story paints a living portrait of the ways in which mistakes can be redeemed to show God's purpose. The youngest of three siblings, Margarita grew up with an alcoholic mother and an abusive stepfather. She tried to tell her mom about the stepfather's abuse, but her mom wouldn't listen. So, when Margarita was 15, she filed for emancipation at the county court. Her mom didn't bother to show up to fight it. A few weeks later, she found out she was pregnant — with her stepfather's child. During her pregnancy, she started dating a 38-year-old man who was fresh out of jail. After she had her son, she found out she was pregnant again at her six-week checkup. Her boyfriend smoked crack and soon, Margarita was joining him. Before she knew, she had recreated the lifestyle in which her mother had raised her.

Margarita remembers every detail of the night her boyfriend cut her throat and stabbed her 37 times. She made dinner for her family and went to lie down on the bed. He came in and crawled on her. She pushed him off, thinking he was playing. He came back a few minutes later, lifted up her head and dragged the knife across the lower portion of her neck. She wasn't sure what was happening at first. But then she felt her neck and then examined her sticky fingertips in the glow of the TV. "You stabbed me," she said in disbelief, as blood poured down her chest. He said nothing. He just stabbed her over and over, 37 times.

She grabbed a blue blanket off the couch and ran for the door, trying to unlock the chain to get out. But she couldn't wiggle it off in time. He stabbed her again and she fainted.

She remembers stumbling around the house, trying to find a phone. The next thing she knew, she was in the back of an ambulance. She was airlifted to University of California-Davis Medical Center, where she flat lined twice. Margarita could not understand why she was alive, but she knows now God had a plan to redeem her life. But as the physical scars began to heal, her soul didn't. Margarita continued to smoke crack, abuse alcohol, and date abusive men to numb the pain. She had several more children and bounced around from California to Washington to Virginia, back to California.

The breaking point came in 1999. Margarita was arrested for stealing her cousin's identity. She calls herself a "dope fiend on a rampage." She got a new birth certificate and Social Security card and wrote bad checks totaling more than $25,000. Arrested, she spent five years and eight months in jail and admits now that "prison saved me." She had a baby while in jail, who was adopted into another family when she was four months old. Her mother passed away. To Margarita, life was not worth living anymore.

After being released, she met another man who abused her and cheated on her. She had three children with him. Her final straw came when she caught him cheating on her in her house. She packed her bags, grabbed her three babies and boarded a plane. The plane landed in Dallas and she went to a domestic violence shelter. The shelter happened to be across the street from our Buckner Family Pathways program.

The day Margarita walked through the door at Buckner, her caseworker remembers that Margarita's "spirit was dark and she looked burdened." Margarita had tried to take her own life shortly before moving to Buckner. She didn't know God, and she didn't understand her purpose in life. When she looked in the mirror, all she could see were the physical scars on her neck and arms that represented the emotional scars on her heart. The healing process had barely begun. During tough times, Margarita would walk up and down a nearby street, where she passed a church. One day, it caught her attention. It was a Saturday morning and some church members were setting up for an event the following day. She watched for a while and continued on her way. All along, she was seeing women in the Buckner program giving their lives to God. The next morning, she went back to the church, where she was welcomed with open arms and as her burdens started to lift, she knew she was home.

Margarita's life was completely redeemed when she accepted Jesus Christ as her Lord and Savior and was baptized. Now, she will tell you that she sees life differently. Her passion is helping other women — and men — who have been in her situation, specifically teens. Margarita isn't as weighed down as she once was. She smiles constantly. She sees the good in people and how she can give to them, not get from them. Every day is a challenge for Margarita as she fights the demons of her past, but she says she's learned that struggle is not always bad. Through years of pain, she had no hope. She felt worthless. But today, she will tell you that redemption to her is overcoming; it is continuing; it is not giving up the fight. She will tell you that living under the guidance and influence of the Holy Spirit and the spiritual power that comes from her relationship with Jesus is what sustains her each day and makes the difference for her new life. For Margarita, redemption means a new life,; a new start. And while she may live with scars both inside and outside her body, she is nonetheless a new creation.

My own story of redemption, though not as dramatic as Margarita's began when I heard my pastor, Bill Thornton, explain God's story of redemption. He spoke of the opportunity to be forgiven, to have my sins wiped away, to enter into God's plan for my life in this world as well as the life to come. I did not think of myself as a terrible person but I knew that I did not measure up to God's standard for holiness and perfection. I was convinced that something had to change and that I could not rely on my own merits, my own efforts, to have a right relationship with God. I needed someone to help me overcome my own humanity, to fill the gap between what I was and what I hoped to be. My pastor clearly explained how I could have forgiveness of my sin. I went home that day after church and after our Sunday lunch I asked my mother how I could have the forgiveness of my sins that the pastor spoke of. I told her that I wanted to be sure that I was forgiven, I wanted to settle the issue of my destination after death, and I wanted to find my purpose in life. She explained how I was a sinner (Romans 3:23); how God made a way for me to be forgiven even when I was not seeking him (Romans 5:8); how my sins led to death and how the death of Jesus for my sins was God's gift to me (Romans 6:23); and how personal faith and trust in Jesus would set me free from sin (Romans 5:8). I asked my mother how I might receive God's gift. She and my father led me to pray and ask Jesus to forgive me, to receive his gift of forgiveness, and to help me find his purpose for my life.

I could not wait until the next Sunday to go back to church and share the good news of my new faith in Jesus with my pastor and the congregation. My story of redemption started in my home with my parents. My story became part of God's story of redemption across the ages. Everything God has in store for me in this life flows out of my recognition that I am a sinner in need of God's grace, in need of redemption, a satisfying of my debt as a sinner, the payment of a ransom of my life from the dominion of darkness to the kingdom of Jesus. This is what redemption means to me. But the story does not end there. Rather, it only begins with forgiveness of sins.

My redemption story is still being written. God is still redeeming all that was stolen, killed, and destroyed in my life for his purpose. He is reversing the lies that came into our family with the truth of who we are in Jesus and for the kingdom. My story includes my own work as an agent of redemption. I treasure the opportunity to offer my gifts, abilities, background, education, experiences, aspirations, and dreams in the service of my redeemer as an instrument, a tool, and a servant advancing the kingdom of the son God loves. My work as a pastor, a business leader, an educational administrator, and as president of a global ministry is focused on how I can serve God's redemptive mission in the lives of vulnerable children, orphans, seniors, and their families. This is what it means to me to live life to its fullest and to be an agent of redemption.

DISCUSSION QUESTIONS

1. After reading Colossians 1:13-14, what stands out the most of the redeeming work of Jesus for you?

2. What does it mean for you to be rescued from the dominion of darkness?

3. If being transferred from the dominion of darkness into the Kingdom of Jesus, what does it mean, in tangible terms, for the Kingdom of God to come near to you and your family?

4. Ultimately, redemption starts with the forgiveness of sin and the transformation of everything about us; and taking the bad and turning it into good for us. How has this happened in your life?

5. How does the theme of this book inform the way you might pray?

TWO:

Redemption in the Old Testament

O Israel, put your hope in the Lord, for with the Lord is unfailing love and with him is full redemption. He himself will redeem Israel from all their sins.

PSALM 130:7-8

"ONE THING I DID [IN THE SHELTER] WAS I PRAYED A LOT."

Shanjula Harris woke up early every morning in the homeless shelter to help her children get ready for school. After she dropped them off, she came back, put on her nicest clothes and started walking. "Every day, Lord knows, I'd walk up and downtown Dallas and ask for work. And I did it every single day," she said. Shanjula had worked for years as a medical assistant at a Dallas hospital, but when she lost her job in 2009, she had nowhere to go. She and her three children — Deon, Precious, and Twquan, were forced to move into a shelter the day before Thanksgiving.

Her story isn't unusual. About 85 percent of homeless families in the United States are headed by women — specifically single women with children. "One thing I did [in the shelter] was I prayed a lot," she said. "There were a lot of things I didn't understand. And some days I didn't feel like praying. But I knew I had to because I knew it wasn't me by myself. I had my kids to think about, too." In 2010, Shanjula received the break she needed: she was accepted into a self-sufficiency family ministry for single parent families seeking higher education in Dallas. She was also offered a new job. She was able to study and work full time, while her children attended school. She graduated with her bachelor's degree in psychology and hopes to someday attend medical school.

Shanjula and her children became part of a "program" that combines housing, day care, and access to college education for residents, who are primarily single mothers. On one level, the program offers redemption from abusive, desperate circumstances these moms and their families face. But on a much higher level, the goal and purpose of the program is holistic redemption of the entire person.

Reflecting on her experience, Shanjula says her life "changed from having nothing to having something. It makes me feel good to know I have a goal set. I wanted my children to see me graduate, to say, 'My mom did it. She was a single parent raising three children by herself. If she can do it, I can do it.'"

Shanjula needed redemption from her circumstances, and she needed a sense of hope for the future. Her redemption began on a spiritual level and later she found full redemption from her circumstances for her, her family, and the next generation. Her world changed as she and her family became part of the story of redemption. She found hope; she experienced God's unfailing love, and she began to write the next chapter in her story of redemption. Her story represents a cosmic transaction in faith and weaves her into God's plan of redemption for her, her family, and everyone in her circle of influence.

From the beginning of human history, God's work and purpose for humanity was to redeem what was lost in the garden. What was intended for harm, over and over again, is made into good through God's work of redemption. In the Old Testament, we can see patterns of his redemptive work in the lives of unsuspecting people. It is in his nature to redeem broken people.

HOW DOES GOD TEACH REDEMPTION TO HIS PEOPLE?

The concept of redemption was taught to God's people, the people of Israel, by relating it to every day life and worship practice. Old Testament writers spoke in terms of financial transactions to explain what God wanted to do in their lives spiritually. In the Old Testament, redemption is used both as a financial and spiritual transaction as an expression of faith. Leviticus 25:24-51 describes redemption in terms of a real estate transaction whereby redemption had to be paid to transfer ownership of land in the context of the year of Jubilee. The year of Jubilee came every 50 years on the Day of Atonement. In the year of Jubilee, all the inhabitants of Israel were to return to his or her own land and arrange for the redemption of their lands by paying redemption money for the land. The passage describes the procedures and regulations involved in the sale of a plot of land by its original owner. If a land owner was not able to redeem himself from his situation and redeem his land, he and his children were to be released in the year of Jubilee (Leviticus 25:54). Jubilee was a year of celebration when debts were forgiven and people were released from difficult circumstances. The concept of redemption was woven into the fabric of economic life and practice.

In Numbers 3:48-51, redemption is described in terms of a financial transaction to account for firstborn males according to Levite priestly tradition. A census was taken of the Levites with an estimate of 22,000 first-born males. However, when the census was complete there were 22,273 with a surplus of 273 firstborn individuals. Redemption was based on the surplus of firstborns at a figure of five shekels paid to the priests per firstborn, or 1,365 shekels. The book of Numbers taught that the firstborn male of each family belonged to God. The needs of the priests in the wilderness were accounted for through redemption of the firstborn males paid to Aaron and his sons. After the period of the exile, the needs of the priesthood were provided for through the redemption for the firstborn.

Leviticus and Numbers show how redemption, as a financial transaction, was woven into the fabric of social and religious aspects of Jewish life. The basic teaching was that provision was made possible through redemption. All the needs we might have are provided for through God's redeeming work in our lives.

In Psalm 130:7-8, the psalmist writes about God's redemption not only from sin but also from difficult circumstances. In this passage, redemption refers to deliverance as a visible sign of divine forgiveness, rather than only the forgiveness of sins. The word for redemption in Hebrew is *padhah*. This word is used to describe redemption beyond sin alone to include deliverance from a tangible and visible menace. The community's hope was in God's total reversal of its problems for those who turned to and trusted in him.[1] The story of redemption is just that — a story, or a collection of stories woven together through salvation history to form our understanding of God's work and purpose, not only in our own lives and personal stories, but throughout the ages. God's redeeming work in our lives goes beyond the spiritual to the practical and real menace in our lives that seek to destroy us. God is able to reverse those situations and turn them into good, for our good, for his glory. The reversal of destructive circumstances and deliverance from a tangible and visible menace can be seen in the stories of Old Testament heroes like Abraham and Isaac, Joseph, Moses, and Ruth, to name a few.

ABRAHAM: REDEEMED THROUGH OBEDIENT FAITH

The story of Abraham's willingness to offer his son Isaac to God illustrates both the transactional and spiritual nature of redemption. It also illustrates for us the kind of faith an agent of redemption needs to find our place in redemptive history.

Imagine praying and waiting for a child, as Abraham and Sara did only to be told by God to "take your son, your only son, whom you love" and sacrifice him as a burnt offering. The burnt offering is a necessary transaction for atonement; the subject of the sacrifice, Isaac, is a test of Abraham's faith and obedience. So Abraham makes the trek as God directs to an unknown destination. How many times has God called you to step out in faith toward an unknown place? Yet Abraham demonstrates the necessary ingredients we must also have if we are to be agents of redemption — trust and obey.

Three days into the journey, Abraham sees the place where God has brought him. He finishes the last part of the journey with only Isaac, placing the burden of carrying the wood on his son. Think about the irony of the sacrifice shouldering the burden of his own impending death. As they make their way up the mountain, Isaac asked his father, "Where is the lamb for the burnt offering?" In a show of true faith, Abraham answers, "God himself will provide the lamb for the burnt offering, my son." *Yahweh Jireh*. God provides. Those two words define redemption. Just as Abraham "reached out his hand and took the knife to slay his son," an angel shouted to him, "Do not lay a hand on the boy." In the thicket nearby, God provided a ram, stuck in the brambles. "He went over and took the ram and sacrificed it as a burnt offering instead of his son."

Abraham's willingness to follow God in obedience and faith to an unknown place to sacrifice his only son foreshadows God's own willingness to provide our redemption through the ultimate sacrifice of his only son. Both are real, tangible transactions with spiritual implications. In this story, we see Abraham's faith and obedience and God's redemption.

JOSEPH: REDEEMED THROUGH SUFFERING

Genesis 37 through 50 chronicles the amazing story of Joseph from his early days as a dreamer through his role as second in command of Egypt under Pharaoh. Joseph experienced mistreatment, injustice, cruelty, and deception throughout his journey. He was sold by his brothers as a slave (Genesis 12-36); he was accused of adultery by the wife of Potiphar, his master, and was unjustly thrown into prison (Genesis 39:1-23); and was forgotten in prison by the cupbearer rather than commending Joseph for release from prison (Genesis 40:23). Finally, Joseph was recognized for his ability to interpret Pharaoh's dreams and was placed in charge of Egypt under Pharaoh. Joseph provided management over Egypt's harvest and led them through seven years of famine. Through this experience he came back in touch with his family and was in a position to reconcile their relationships. Joseph was instrumental not only in saving their lives through the famine but also playing a role in God's redeeming work in his life, his family, and the entire nation of Israel.

The story of Joseph teaches us several principles of redemption. First, nothing can stop God's redemptive plans for our lives. Second, God's redemptive plan for our lives may not exclude pain, injustice, false accusations, or mistreatment. Redemption does not mean a life exempt of pain, hurt, mistreatment, or injustice. Third, the redeeming God is able to reverse tangible problems, destructive circumstances, and extremely harsh situations for his redemptive purpose and glory.

In the final chapter of Genesis, we read of the death of Jacob, Joseph's father. At the news of their father's death, Joseph's brothers began to fear they would receive what they deserved — retribution, punishment, imprisonment, and perhaps death as a result of a feared grudge that Joseph might present. They had no escape, no way out, no ransom, no leverage, no negotiating power. All they had left was the hope of mercy and grace through repentance. They sent word to Joseph with instructions found in the last words of their father, Jacob. From the grave, his father's words would speak to Joseph: "I ask you to forgive your brothers the sins and the wrongs they committed in treating you so badly" (Genesis 50:17). When Joseph heard these words, he began to cry. The story of redemption gets better and the plot thickens at this point. His brothers come in to the palace, gain an audience with their brother, throw themselves at the feet of Joseph, and announce, "we are your slaves." The brothers who sold Joseph into slavery as a young man now reverse their roles and throw themselves into slavery hoping for the best. Joseph immediately reassures his brothers and tells them not to be afraid and reinterprets the story of his life, their lives, and he reveals the plot of the redemption story: "You intended to harm me, but God intended it for good to accomplish what is now being done, the saving of many lives. So then, do not be afraid. I will provide for you and your children" (Genesis 50:20).

At the age of 110, Joseph gathered his brothers and told them he was about to die. Even at the point of his death, Joseph spoke of God's continuing redemption story. He said, "But God will surely come to your aid and take you up out of this land to the land he promised on oath to Abraham, Isaac, and Jacob" (Genesis 50:24). How can a person so mistreated and maligned like Joseph forgive? What was it about him that gave him the strength to restore, preserve, serve, and protect the lives of those who wanted him dead? It has to come from Joseph's relationship with God as redeemer. Those who trust and hope in the Lord for his redemptive purpose are able to say with Joseph "You intended to harm me, but God intended it for good to accomplish what is now being done, the saving of many lives" (Genesis 50:21). The lives of the redeemed become tools in the hands of the redeemer. Do you have the courage and strength to say this to the person that may have hurt you?

MOSES: REDEEMED TO REDEEM

The book of Exodus starts a new chapter in the life of the people of Israel when "a new king, who did not know about Joseph, came to power in Egypt" (Exodus 1:8). The people of Israel were turned into slaves rather than valued citizens of Egypt. As slaves, they were oppressed and forced into slave labor used to build the cities of Pithom and Ramses as store cities for Pharaoh. The King of Egypt ruthlessly ordered that all male Hebrew children be put to death at the hand of midwives. The newborn boys were to be thrown in the Nile River. When Moses was born, his mother placed him in a basket in the Nile River. Pharaoh's daughter went down to the Nile to bathe and found Moses in the basket. She sent her servant to draw him out; find the boy's mother to nurse him; and later adopted Moses as her own son (Exodus 2).

Moses grew up as an educated Egyptian leader. One day he saw an Egyptian beating a Hebrew slave. Moses became frustrated with the abuse of his people and in a moment of rage, he killed the Egyptian task master who was beating the Hebrew slave. Moses then tried to hide what he had done by burying the Egyptian in the sand. When he realized word had spread about the murder, Pharaoh tried to apprehend Moses to kill him. But Moses fled to the desert of Midian. There he met Jethro and married Zipporah, one of Jethro's daugthers.

One day while Moses was tending Jethro's flock on the far side of the desert near the mountain of Horeb, an angel of the Lord appeared to Moses in flames of fire within a bush. Moses went closer to see what was causing the bush to burn but not be consumed. As he came closer he heard a voice saying, "I am the God of your father, the God of

Abraham, the God of Isaac and the God of Jacob." God continued to speak to Moses saying that Moses was to go back to Egypt to tell Pharaoh to let God's people go free (Exodus 3).

If you were Moses, at this point in your life, how would you feel if God found you on the far side of the desert? Moses was afraid, and I would be too if I thought I had gotten away with murder. Moses probably thought his life was over and finished due to the murder he committed. God called Moses to deliver and set free the people of Israel from injustice, bondage, and oppression, and he wanted Moses to lead the way. Moses responded by providing a long list of disqualifiers and excuses. God reminded him that Moses would be going in God's name: "I am who I am" sent him (Exodus 3:14). Moses would eventually lead the people out of Egypt, across the Red Sea, across the desert where he would receive the Ten Commandments, and toward the Promised Land (Exodus 13-40).

When we feel disqualified from anything good in our lives, God qualifies us, not on our merits, but on his. When we think we are qualified, we probably aren't. God doesn't call qualified people into his service; rather, he qualifies those he calls. This is the turning point of redemption for Moses. God found Moses to use him for his redemptive purpose in history. Sometimes the bad things that happen to us are consequences of poor decisions we have made. Sometimes, in our effort to serve God, we can get ahead of him and take matters into our own hands, literally. Yet, the God of redemption is not limited by our mistakes. He has a larger story in mind that can overcome our shortcomings in order to fulfill his purpose. He is the God of the great reversal in our lives. What might be intended for harm, God intends it for good. That's why often our story isn't finished as soon we might think. God just might have another chapter.

RUTH: REDEEMED THROUGH PERSONAL LOSS AND GRIEF

The story of Ruth and Boaz in the book of Ruth was shaped by the law found in Deuteronomy 24:19-22 regarding the practice of gleaning. In Deuteronomy, Moses is speaking to the children of slaves. His audience represents the next generation poised to move into the land they learned about as children. Keep in mind, that Moses led a whole generation of slaves out of Egypt, across the Red Sea, into the desert, gave them the law, and now pauses, just this side of the Jordan River as the next generation prepares to cross into prosperity and blessing. The 24th chapter of Deuteronomy records Moses' instructions from his last words regarding the fatherless, the widow, and the alien. He issues a call to justice, a call to generosity, and a call to redemption.

Ruth, a Moabite woman[2], could be considered an orphan since she was not with her family. She was a widow and she was an alien in a foreign land. Her mother-in-law, Naomi suffered the loss of her husband; then Ruth and Orpha both suffered the loss of their husbands while living in Moab. Naomi decided to move back to Bethlehem and Ruth went with her. While back in Bethlehem, Naomi instructs Ruth to glean wheat in the fields. She realizes later that she was gleaning in the fields belonging to Boaz, a man of high standing in the community. Boaz instructs his workers to leave part of the field un-harvested and allows Ruth to glean from the fields for survival. Ruth later marries Boaz and is brought into the story of redemption. Boaz becomes her "kinsman redeemer." He buys the land belonging to Naomi and Ruth and provides for Ruth. Boaz and Ruth became the parents of Obed, who became the father of Jesse, the father of King David, a true son of Judah and an ancestor to Joseph, the father of Jesus. You never know who you are helping in God's redemptive work.

Who has not known the loss of a loved one through death? We are all impacted by the loss of life. Sometimes the loss is sudden and sometimes the loss is gradual. Some of us have experienced the loss of a spouse; suddenly you become a widow or widower. Some of us have suffered the loss of parents and family; some losses come to us when we are children; and others have experienced the loss of one's home-land through immigration to another country. The story of Ruth reminds us that even in our loss God is working out a way to redeem our experience and our lives for his purposes. If we perceive our loss only through human eyes, it may appear that God is not anywhere to be found. One author says God is everywhere but totally hidden in purely human coincidences and schemes...God's providential work is his "hiddenness."[3] Redemption is sometimes God's hidden guidance woven into the fabric of everyday life even if you are a widow, an orphan, or an alien. Your loss may have been intended for harm but God intends it for good.

Natasha Potts is someone who was lost, hidden among more than 1 million orphans in Russia. But one day a group of Americans showed up at her orphanage with the most unlikely of gifts — a new pair of shoes. The next time you put on a pair of shoes, think about Natasha's story and remember that for this lost and hidden child, a new pair of shoes was, in her own words, transformational. "Receiving a pair of shoes was one of the happiest moments in my life." Think about that. How do you feel when you put on a new pair of shoes? If you're honest, you probably don't feel anything. "I had something that someone thought enough of me to provide them just for me," she said. But in God's providence, Natasha's new shoes were only the beginning. For what started with a simple gift of shoes became a forever family when Bob and Donita Potts adopted her and brought Natasha, a hidden and lost orphan, into their home in the United States. God's work of redemption continues today in her life, for when it may have seemed to Natasha that God was nowhere to be found, he was there, in the hiddenness.

DISCUSSION QUESTIONS

1. Reading Psalm 130:7-8, how have you experienced God's unfailing love and full redemption?

2. If redemption is God's great reversal in the lives of those he loves, what has he reversed from bad to good in your life?

3. From Abraham's life, what do you observe about the relationship between obedience and redemption? How does this story move you to engage in redemptive living?

4. What observations do you have about Joseph's story? How has God taken what was intended to harm you and turned it into good?

5. What does the story of Moses teach us about God's redemptive work?

6. How has God's redemptive work been hidden and revealed in your life?

THREE:

REDEMPTION IN THE NEW TESTAMENT

He redeemed us in order that the blessing given to Abraham might come to the Gentiles through Christ Jesus, so that by faith we might receive the promise of the Spirit.

GALATIANS 3:14

"I WOULD NOT HAVE KNOWN WHAT IT WAS TO LOVE JESUS AND MY SOUL WOULD HAVE BEEN LOST."

In 1883 a little girl came to live at Buckner Orphans Home in Dallas, Texas founded by Dr. Robert Cook Buckner. She came with "morals badly impaired and language shocking." Mrs. S. A. Reese was one of the matrons charged with caring for the orphan girls. The child was dealt with kindly and firmly. One night when Dr. Buckner had offered prayer and it was now time to send the children to bed, the little girl threw her arms about her matron's neck, her big brown eyes streaming with tears, and exclaimed, "O Mamma Reese, if I had not come into this home, what would have become of my soul? I would not have known what it was to love Jesus and my soul would have been lost."[1]

Since the very beginning of the ministry of Buckner, the under-current of this social service ministry has been the redemption of lives for God's purpose. In the context of a loving family environment marked by the life and teachings of Jesus of Nazareth, a little girl in need of a family found a home. But the story does not end there. She also found the love of Jesus and a personal relationship with him and was grafted into the family of faith. Her story and the stories of thousands across the generations dispel what was once traditional thought — that social ministry and evangelism were by nature mutually exclusive. Like many in my generation, I was raised believing that redemption was a one-sided coin; that the message of salvation was essentially a fire insurance policy from hell, even if a person was living in hell on earth. But along the way in my growth as a follower of Jesus, I've come to realize that the practical impact of the gospel and the gospel message of salvation cannot be separated, like two sides of the same coin. Or as Dr. Boyd Hunt writes in his book, *Redeemed! Eschatological Redemption and the Kingdom of God,* "The goal of God's kingdom mission in Christ is nothing less than to bring *all things* into subjection to Christ (Col. 1:20). God's redemptive intent is comprehensive and wholistic." Personal faith in Jesus as your redeemer goes far beyond solving the spiritual problem we have with sin. Redemption involves conforming everything about us into the purpose God has for our lives to bless us and those around us according to his plan in redemptive history for us and others around us.

The biblical concept of salvation relates to our need as sinners for a savior. Jesus Christ, the Lord is the savior I am referring to in familiar verses like John 3:16. For God so loved the world that he gave his only son that whoever believes in him will not perish but have everlasting life. That life is in God's son, Jesus. It is through his life, work, death, burial, and resurrection that our salvation is secured. We come to faith in Jesus by trusting in him to forgive our sins on the basis of his work and not on anything we have done. We serve him not as a means to win his favor but as an expression for his love and grace toward us. It was at our point of defiance to God that he sent his son to die for us. So, we live in effort to demonstrate our thanks to him for what he has done for us. There is a redeeming aspect in our salvation and yet our salvation is much broader and deeper than redemption. Redemption speaks to what happens to us at the point of our salvation but also reaches backward to the pain of our lives and forward to show us how the redeemer makes all things new and how that newness connects with what God is doing in human history. We are saved by our savior and redeemed by our redeemer who calls us into action and full-time service for his purposes in redemptive history.

THE THEME OF REDEMPTION IN THE NEW TESTAMENT

E. F. Harrison said, "No word in Christian vocabulary deserves to be held more precious than Redeemer, for even more than Savior it reminds the child of God that his salvation has been purchased at a great and personal cost, for the Lord has given himself for our sins in order to deliver us from them."[2] As a child I understood Jesus as my savior but as an adult I have come to understand him more deeply as my redeemer. I have lived long enough to experience Jesus as both savior and redeemer of my life. Theologian Otto Webber, asserts that God's self-disclosure is both reconciliation and redemption through the life, death, and resurrection of Jesus of Nazareth.[3] The concept of redemption is found throughout the New Testament.

The New Testament was written in the first century in the Mediterranean world during the Greco-Roman civilization. As such, the common language was Koine Greek. In order to fully understand the concept of redemption in the New Testament, I will use a number of Greek words and give their meaning in English. The two Greek words that are used most often for redemption in the New Testament are *exagorazo* and *lutrosis*.[4] *Exagorazo*, meaning to buy, buy out, especially when purchasing a slave with a view to his freedom, is used in Galatians, Ephesians, Colossians, and Revelation.[5] *Lutrosis*, meaning to release on receipt of ransom; by paying a ransom, is used in Luke, Romans, Ephesians, Colossians, 1 Corinthians, Titus, 1 Peter, and Hebrews.[6] The root word for *exagorazo* is *agora*, meaning "market, to buy." This was used in the New Testament to indicate commercial life. In the previous chapter, I mentioned how the word for redemption was also tied to a financial transaction. In the New Testament, *exagorazo* is used for the redeeming and liberating act of Christ. This word also means an intensive buying which exhausts the possibilities available.[7] The New Testament use of this word for the work of Christ on the cross denotes a divine transaction that exhausts all means possible to gain our freedom through the sacrifice of Jesus for us. The root word for *lutrosis* is *luo*, meaning "to loose" and is used for the freeing of slaves. The noun form of this word translates as "ransom" and also carries the meaning of "money paid to ransom prisoners of war." The verses in Matthew 20:28 and Mark 10:45 both speak of the idea that Jesus came to give his life as a ransom for many. The understanding is that Jesus' death as a ransom for us is a basic element in the Church's confession that cannot be surrendered. The New Testament carries this central idea when referring to the concept of redemption.[8] Stories of the redemptive work of Jesus are found throughout the New Testament. The theme of redemption comes into sharp focus in the lives of three stories of ordinary people living in the first century during the time of Jesus. Each person's life was transformed completely and wholly by the work of Jesus through redemption. Let's focus on the stories of Zacchaeus, the Samaritan woman at the well, and the Philippian jailer.

STORIES OF REDEMPTION IN THE NEW TESTAMENT

When I thought about three stories to illustrate redemption in the New Testament, I struggled with whom to select. I thought about Peter and Paul, but I decided on Zacchaeus, the Samaritan woman at the well, and the Philippian jailer because these are everyday people beyond the 12 disciples and Paul the apostle. In a sense, these three people are easy to relate to. Their stories represent the bright hope of redemption for all of us. My hope is that your story will somehow connect with these three redeemed people, but more importantly that you connect with the Redeemer who makes all things new.

ZACCHAEUS: REDEEMED IN THE MARKETPLACE

The story of Zacchaeus is recorded in Luke chapter 19. Jesus made his entrance into Jericho where Zacchaeus, a tax collector lived. Zacchaeus heard about Jesus and wanted to see him so he found a sycamore tree to climb up to enable a better view of Jesus as he entered the city. When Jesus reached the spot where Zacchaeus was he said to him, "Zacchaeus, come down immediately. I must stay at your house today." That is a pretty amazing encounter. Jesus knows his name, calls him by name, and invites himself to stay at his house. Now fast forward to later in the evening at dinner. The next thing we see in the story is Zacchaeus rising to his feet, apparently in the middle of dinner, to say, "Look, Lord! Here and now I give half of my possessions to the poor, and if I have cheated anybody out of anything, I will pay back four times the amount." Wow! Did you see that? Jesus then says to Zacchaeus, "Today salvation has come to this house, because this man, too, is a son of Abraham. For the Son of Man came to seek and to save what was lost."

I don't know what the table talk was like that evening as they reclined to eat in Mediterranean style. The vocation of Zacchaeus was among the most hated and reviled at that time in history. In that day, tax collectors had the notorious reputation for stealing from everyone through the taxes they collected. A tax collector was not to be trusted but instead was to be held in contempt and hated. So what would Jesus have been talking about that caused Zacchaeus to stand up in the middle of dinner and say, "Look, Lord!"? Did Jesus talk about the Kingdom of God, his love for Zacchaeus, stewardship, financial principles, sin, and forgiveness? Did Jesus talk about serving the poor, serving the least of these?

We do not have the details of the conversation but we know the response. My working assumption is that they are having dinner when Zacchaeus stood up. The word *statheis* describes a formal act, as one who is about to make a formal declaration.[9] Zacchaeus first said, "Look" as though he wanted to prove or demonstrate something to Jesus. Then he said, "Lord!" With that word he was saying "Jesus, you are the master of my life and everything I have." Then he made a commitment that very day, that very moment, to give half of his possessions to the poor and he made an open ended declaration that if anyone felt cheated he would pay them back four-fold to make things right. So, how does that happen over a dinner conversation?

Jesus gave us a hint into what happened to Zacchaeus. Salvation came to the heart of this tax collector. He had an on-the-spot turn around in his heart, mind, and soul. In biblical language we call this "repentance." It even reached his pocket book. All that was intended to harm Zacchaeus and those he had harmed was now reversed. All things were made right and redeemed for good. From that day forward he would never be the same.

Zacchaeus entered into a redeeming relationship with Jesus. It was as though Jesus released him from the grip of selfishness and personal gain. Jesus liberated Zacchaeus for the life he was intended to live. It was as though Zacchaeus was a slave to selfishness but then freed to live generously. His new freedom caused him to re-think how he was living his life and to reconsider what should be different from that moment forward. Zacchaeus knew he was forgiven and that simple truth changed everything.

Redemption does that to you. Restitution is good proof of a changed heart and required by Mosaic Law. Redeemed people know they have been forgiven and make commitments to make things right. What is it about your life that needs to be made right as a redeemed person? Who, in your life, do you need to make contact with, to make things right, to straighten out a relationship, a business transaction, or to right a wrong? When you do this, people around you will notice the difference the Jesus makes in your life. Redemptive transformation will not only change your life, but that of your family, neighbors, co-workers, and friends. This is the power of the Redeemer working in you. And the impact of redemptive transformation changes every part of who you are.

THE SAMARITAN WOMAN AT THE WELL: REDEEMED AS A BRIDGE TO HER COMMUNITY

The story of the Samaritan woman at the well near Sychar is found in the fourth chapter of the Gospel of John. Jesus has just left Judea in southern Palestine where he had gained many followers. He decided to leave this area and travel north, back to Galilee. The normal navigational route for any self-respecting Jew was the trans-Jordan route to the north. In order to avoid the region of Samaria, Jews would head east through Jericho to cross to the east side of the Jordan River in order to travel north through Perea and then cross back over to the west side of the river north of Samaria near Gadara to head back to Galilee. Cultural hostilities between Jews and Samaritans can be traced back to 931 BC through the New Testament period as recorded in John chapter four. Samaritans emerged as a distinct ethnic group as described in Second Kings 17. Samaritans claimed to be descendants of the tribe of

Joseph and the descendants of Ephraim and Manasseh. Jews rejected them because they intermarried with Assyrian colonists. Samaritans were a product of a blending or mixture of Jewish and Canaanite peoples. The forbidden intermarriage produced a people who were rejected and despised. This new cultural group called Samaritans gave birth to a distinct worldview that was at odds with a Jewish worldview.

When John records that Jesus "had to go through Samaria," he was making an astonishing statement. No Jew in his right mind would travel through Samaria. Certainly no Jew would feel he "had" to go through Samaria. This was a countercultural statement in the day of Jesus. Yet he was driven by a sense of mission, passion, and vision to go through Samaria. Over the course of the conversation, Jesus responds to the Samaritan woman's agenda regarding culture, history, and religion. She brought the pain of her past into the conversation. Culturally, she would question the social appropriateness of a male Jew speaking with a Samaritan woman in Samaria. Historically, she raised the reference point of Jacob as the father of the Samaritans. Religiously, she pointed to the correctness of the place of worship. Jesus gently acknowledged the cultural pain of her past; he points beyond history to the spiritual issue of the moment; and he points beyond places of worship to the issue of spirit and truth as qualifications for true worshippers rather than location. Jesus was interested in the redemptive potential of her life, as seen in the shift in conversation.

He gradually disclosed his identity by raising the issue of her husbands and the man she was currently with. Over the course of the conversation, she first knew Jesus as a man, then as a Jewish man, then as a prophet, and finally as Messiah. Once she realized that Jesus was not just a Jewish man or a prophet, but the Messiah (the Christ), she sped back to the town of Sychar leaving her water jar in place. Something had happened in her heart. She went back to town to tell everyone she knew to "Come and see a man who told me everything I ever did. Could this be the Christ?" John records that many of the Samaritans from that town believed in him (Jesus) because of what the Samaritan woman said about the man that "told me everything I ever did" but many more became believers after they heard Jesus for themselves. They said to the Samaritan woman, "We no longer believe just because of what you said; now we have heard for ourselves and we know that this man really is the Savior of the world."

The Samaritan woman's life was redeemed from a series of failed marriages, adultery, social stigmatism, cultural conflict and the negative impact of this kind of lifestyle. She was trapped in the prison of social stigmatism in her day. She was a slave to her own failures and search for happiness. She needed to be free from the depths of pain in her life. One encounter with Jesus, who did not condemn her but showed her the way to a better life, transformed her into a witness that led many from her town to faith in Christ. Jesus liberated her to a new purpose in life. We see a major reversal in this woman's life. Jesus, the Redeemer, was able to take a life torn by the consequences of sin and transform her relationships and circle of influence into a magnet that led others to faith. He took what was intended for harm and turned it into good. The redemptive work of Jesus cuts across all social strata, cultural differences, gender differences, and geography. What might be the redemptive potential of your life? How does God want to use you for his work in redemptive history?

THE PHILIPPIAN JAILER: REDEEMED FOR FAMILY AND COMMUNITY

The story of the Philippian jailer is recorded in Acts 16, written by Luke, the physician and follower of Jesus. Dr. Thom Wolf once characterized the Philippian jailer as someone you would not want to meet in a dark alley at night. Wolf said, "Roman soldiers never die, they simply retire at Philippi." Now a jailer, he had proven his loyalty to the Roman government as a soldier, a professional warrior. He was highly experienced in the art of war, the heat of battle and the ability to annihilate his enemy in ways that would shock most of us. That is what hand-to-hand battle in the first century was like. The Philippian jailer was a decorated veteran that had been awarded a plush jailer position.

Paul and Silas, followers of Jesus, had been seized and thrown in prison for casting out a demon from a possessed girl. The girl's owners were using her for financial gain because of her fortune-telling abilities. Once Paul and Silas cast out the demon in her she was no longer able to tell fortunes. The men who owned her as a slave were furious with the work of Paul and Silas that ended their business venture so they took them before the authorities and had them thrown into prison. They had them severely flogged for "advocating customs unlawful for Romans to accept or practice."

About midnight, Paul and Silas were praying and singing when an earthquake shook the city and the prison, in particular. All the prison doors flew open and all the prisoners' chains came loose. The jailer, having just woken up, was sure that all the prisoners had escaped or were going to escape, so he quickly came to the conclusion that this would be a dishonor and that the best solution was to end his life. But Paul shouted, "Don't harm yourself! We are all here!" The jailer called for lights, rushed in and fell trembling before Paul and Silas. He brought them out of the prison and asked, "Sirs, what must I do to be saved?" They replied, "Believe in the Lord Jesus, and you will be saved — you and your household."

What happens next is an incredible story of redemptive transformation. The next scene Luke describes is Paul and Silas speaking the word of the Lord to everyone in the jailer's household. The jailer's house must have been above the jail, as was the Roman custom in the first century. Then, the most astonishing thing happened. The jailer who had inflicted the wounds on Paul and Silas was now washing them in the fountain of the inner court of his home with the whole family watching. What could have his children and wife been thinking as they saw this happen? They knew their father as a tough military man but had never seen him as a caring person. They saw the transformation of their father happening right before their eyes. The next thing Luke records is just as astonishing. At that very hour, the jailer and his whole family were baptized. Wow! How did that happen? The only thing I can think of was that they saw the transformational power of redemption taking place in high definition in their father and felt compelled to follow his example. The story of the jailer's redeemed life does not stop with washing wounds or the celebration of baptism for him and his family. It gets even better.

How long does it take for Paul and Silas to be escorted from prison into the jailer's home above the prison to be introduced to the jailer's family, to hear the word of the Lord; to have their wounds washed by the jailer; and then to baptize the jailer and his family? I am thinking it is probably one or two in the morning since everything started at midnight with the earthquake. Next, it is time to celebrate so the jailer brought Paul and Silas, his former prisoners, into his house and set a meal before them. Luke says the jailer was "filled with joy because he had come to believe in God — he and his whole family." Don't miss the detail in this story. The jailer, a decorated Roman soldier, has moved from suicide to service; from inflicting wounds to healing them; from housing alleged criminals in prison to hosting new friends at his dinner table.

How does this happen in the first century? How does this happen in the 21st century? I have seen redemption take place in the lives of scores of people of all kinds of cultures, languages, socio-economic strata, and nationalities. Redemptive transformation, the kind of all-encompassing, life-changing impact that happens when a person finds faith in Jesus is unmistakable and undeniable. Only the power and presence of Jesus can change a hardened person like the jailer. Once his family saw the transformation with their own eyes, they also believed. This jailer would never be the same again. All the difficult experiences of his past as a soldier were at one moment reversed into a life of redeeming transformation. He was not only changed by the power of Jesus, but he became a magnet to draw his family to the way of Jesus. Jesus liberated him from a path of near self-destruction, from suicide, and death to life. The story of the ransom paid by Jesus on the cross led the jailer to freedom through the imprisonment of Paul and Silas. The jailer was free to live a new life in Christ.

Don't miss this important trend in these stories of redemption. The redemption stories of Zacchaeus, the Samaritan woman at the well, and the Philippian jailer have a common thread. Redemption does not stop with them; it goes through them to others. In a sense, they became agents of redemption leading others in their circle of influence to experience the love and power of Jesus the redeemer. Each of these three individuals came to saving faith in Jesus. They came to understand the life Jesus gave as a ransom for theirs, a freedom from captivity, and the opportunity to live free from sin and bondage. They were redeemed and empowered to share this good news with others. I believe with all my heart that this kind of liberating freedom is also available to anyone, regardless of class, race, or socio-economic status. I also believe that resident within every human, regardless of your background and past experience, is a divine redemptive potential for a purposeful life in God's economy of redemption. There is nothing in your life beyond the redemptive reach of Jesus to reverse and turn it into good for his purpose. Redeemed people become agents of redemption; active in God's redeeming work in their generation.

What, then, is an agent of redemption? What does an agent of redemption look like in the 21st century?

DISCUSSION QUESTIONS

1. Reading Galatians 3:14, how is my redemption meant to serve others?

2. How is the theme of redemption central to the Christian faith?

3. What surprises you most about the redemptive experience of Zacchaeus?

4. What surprises you most about the redemptive experience of the Samaritan woman?

5. What stands out most about the redemptive experience of the Philippian jailer?

FOUR:

What is an Agent of Redemption?

"Religion that God our Father accepts as pure and faultless is this: to look after orphans and widows in their distress and to keep oneself from being polluted by the world."

JAMES 1:27

"NOT ONE ORPHAN CHILD...BUT ALL ORPHAN CHILDREN."

What is an agent of redemption? An agent of redemption is a person that has experienced the redeeming love of the good news of Jesus of Nazareth. He or she has been forgiven and is indwelt by the Holy Spirit. An agent of redemption has first experienced his or her own spiritual transfer from a life of bondage to and guilt from sin to the place of repentance, forgiveness, grace, and freedom. An agent of redemption is first and foremost a follower of Jesus; a disciple of Jesus; one whose heart intends to serve Jesus as master every day in an effort to bring glory, to shed light on Jesus the King through one's actions, words, attitudes, vocation, recreation, and relationships. Follow me as I explore this concept further and then offer a working definition.

An agent of redemption has a personal calling to actively engage with people in his or her circle of influence to demonstrate a transformed life and to work, pray, and focus on the redemptive potential in everyone around them. An agent of redemption looks for ways God would want to turn what was meant for harm into good. An agent of redemption knows that the gospel that came to them must go through them to others around them.

An agent of redemption is on a personal mission to pray, work, and hope for the kingdom to come near in this life. This person lives the prayer of Jesus that says "...your kingdom come, your will be done on earth as it is in heaven." An agent of redemption looks at his family, in his neighborhood, in her community, in her city, in her county, in her state, in her nation, and in the world to ask what is it about this place that could look more like the Kingdom of God, right here, right now?

Finally, an agent of redemption sees the world from a unique set of lenses, a Jesus-shaped worldview. An agent of redemption sees this life as temporary, this place as not his or her permanent home. This person lives life in view of eternity and the life to come. An agent of redemption thinks differently from other people. His or her thoughts are not conformed to the pattern of this world; rather, he or she has been transformed by the renewing of the mind.[1] An agent of redemption thinks like Jesus because he or she "has the mind of Christ."[2] In order words, he or she will think about the world and see the world through the mind and eyes of Jesus.

The word "agent" has its origins in Greek, meaning "to drive, to lead." An agent is "something that produces or is capable of producing an effect; an active or efficient cause." A further definition is "one who acts for or in the place of another by authority from him." The word has been used in governments for a representative or emissary. Now, take all of those aspects of the definition and put them into the context of scripture and of the Christian's life and responsibility. We are agents of redemption — God's agents of his redemption. And we act upon his authority and as his representatives. Only Jesus does the work of redemption, yet we are his hands and feet.

It may be helpful to offer a concise definition of an agent of redemption at this point. An agent of redemption is a person of courage, compassion, and conviction on mission with Jesus to turn what was intended for harm into good.

PEOPLE OF COURAGE, COMPASSION, AND CONVICTION

For almost the last 25 years of my life, my way of thinking, and my worldview has been radicalized by a basic teaching I had somehow missed, although not in its entirety, from all the learning, teaching, and exposure to Holy Scripture through Bible study and graduate theological education. Once I came in contact with this form of teaching in the Bible, I could not un-learn it. The pattern, now very clear and obvious to me, permeated my relationships, my ministry, and those I worked with once I became aware of the basic code in the Scripture.

I first came across the teaching in the early 1990s when I visited a medium-sized church on a side street in East Los Angeles. Once I studied the pattern of teaching more deeply, I applied it to my life and ministry and later obtained permission to build a course around this teaching at Baptist University of the Américas in San Antonio, Texas.

About a decade later, while in a doctoral leadership program at Andrews University, I learned that Dr. Thom Wolf had made this basic teaching the core of his research and the subject of his dissertation. We were colleagues in the doctor of philosophy program in Global Leadership at Andrews University in Berrien Springs, Michigan. While I am unable to replicate the study here, I would like to highlight some of the key findings of his study since it serves as a foundational reference point for the idea of an agent of transformation.

Wolf's study magnificently wove together fragments and patterns of Scripture that linked the moral teachings of Jesus and those of the early church with rabbinical teachings of the Diaspora (the dispersion of the Jewish community outside of Israel in the sixth century B.C.) referred to as the three-fold diaspora apologetic. Wolf, quoting Andrew Heffern from a 1915 John Bohlen Lectureship in Philadelphia, advanced the idea that the "three-fold framework of Paul and the earliest congregations have the same framing as the Diaspora three-fold template."[3] The three-fold moral template centered on a worship of God; a moral way of life; and a coming judgment of the world by God.[4]

Wolf calls this three-fold moral template "the Micah Mandate" taken from Micah 6:8, to do justice, love mercy, and walk humbly before your God. He points to Heffern's work as placing "Jesus' own three-fold confirmation that he himself is the way, the truth, and the life within the same Jewish tradition, employing the Diaspora apologetic, the interpretive framework of the three necessary things."[5] In intriguing fashion, Wolf linked Micah's do justice/love mercy/walk humbly[6] and Jesus' justice/mercy/faithfulness[7] with Paul's faith/love/hope[8] triad. Wolf arrived at this linkage by looking backward through Paul's eyes viewing Micah and Jesus through a rear-view mirror so that the order of justice/mercy/faithfulness of Micah and Jesus becomes the faith/love/hope of Paul.

"In a not-right world, the justice/mercy/walk-humbly-before-God triad becomes not just a moral criterion for convictions, compassion, and courage but also a personal, relational, and social critique. Across cultures and time periods, the wholeness of the justice/mercy/walk-humbly triad is remarkably recognized as proper and good; right and complete, comforting and condemning, never to be accomplished, and yet, once heard, never to be forgotten."[9] Wolf calls his triad The

Pattern, the prophetic moral standard for humanity, "the moral syllabus of humanity."[10] It is this core teaching of faith (conviction), love (compassion), and hope (courage) that forms the basic framework of an agent of redemption. An agent of redemption is compelled by his or her faith (conviction), to share God's love in a practical way (compassion), and point to hope (courage) in the most difficult of human circumstances. The agent of redemption is a person of conviction, compassion, and courage.

Rudolph Bultmann, on the ethics of the Apostle Paul, says "all other worldview systems followed the pattern of imperative/indicative: Do this ritual and you will attain this reward…the common imperative/indicative order found in other world religions is uniquely reversed in the logic of earliest Christianity." The oikoscode pattern is indicative/imperative: Because you have already attained a new life standing, let this be your new lifestyle expression. The Apostle Paul's letter to the Galatians 5:25 points to this paradoxical logic which says "Since we live by the Spirit, let us keep in step with the Spirit."[11] In other words, we don't do good because we are good, we do good because we have been redeemed and led by his Spirit to engage in his redemptive plan for humanity. It did not take me long to come up with the best example that personified The Pattern as an agent of redemption. The name of one person in the 20th century stands out as an exemplary example of an agent of redemption: Dr. Robert Cooke Buckner. He was a person of compassion, conviction, and courage who was on mission with Jesus to turn what was intended for him into good.

DR. ROBERT COOKE BUCKNER, AGENT OF REDEMPTION

These words: "Not one orphan child…but all orphan children," are the etched epitaph on the tombstone of Dr. Robert Cooke Buckner. His tombstone is in the center of a simple burial plot in east Dallas in the

Oak Grove Cemetery. These final words capture the essence of an agent of redemption, par excellence, and founder of the Buckner Orphan's Home in Dallas, Texas. If I were to select one shining contemporary example of what it means to be an agent of redemption, I would choose Dr. Buckner, called "Father Buckner" by the orphans because of his role as a father to them. His life story has been the object of at least one book and one dissertation. I will not try to tell his whole life's story here but I will provide some brief headlines from his life and work to paint a picture of what it means to be an agent of redemption and how Robert Cooke Buckner is a shining example of conviction, compassion, and courage.

James 1:27 was the thematic verse that shaped the ministry of Father Buckner. He held high the vision of James which says: "Religion that God our Father accepts as pure and faultless is this: to look after orphans and widows in their distress and to keep oneself from being polluted by the world." While this verse gives us much insight as to what drove him, there is much more to learn about his life story. Who he was, what kind of world he inherited, what he believed, and what he did helps explain why I consider him to be an agent of redemption, par excellence.

WHO WAS ROBERT COOKE BUCKNER?

The Buckner family, of English origin, moved to America before the Revolutionary War and participated in the struggle for independence from England. Robert Cooke Buckner was born in Madisonville, Tennessee, the son of a Baptist pastor, church planter, and denominational leader.[12] He studied Greek, Latin, and Law and received two honorary doctorates, a Doctor of Divinity from Keachi College in Louisiana and a Doctor of Laws from Baylor University. He became a pastor at the age of 17, serving as the pastor of the Somerset Baptist Church in Kentucky. At the age of 20, he became pastor of the Albany Baptist Church in Albany, Kentucky and later became the pastor of the First Baptist Church of Owensboro, Kentucky and pastor of the Salvisa Baptist Church before he moved to Texas.[13] Buckner spent the first nine years of his pastoral ministry in Kentucky and then moved to Texas to serve as a pastor at the age of 26.

When Buckner moved to Paris, Texas in 1859, a Baptist named Sam Houston was running for governor. By 1861 Buckner became the pastor of First Baptist Church of Paris and by 1868 he became a home missionary for the Baptist General Association in a role to advance missions. He spent that year preaching, church planting, and strengthening churches and associations, and saw 159 baptisms, 4 Sunday schools established, and 3 churches established. He did this without a salary.[14] His vision and passion led him to reach out to local churches across the state and from the early years of his life, his willingness to serve and activate his fellow churchmen and churchwomen was obvious. He seemed to be pursuing a calling rather than a career.

On January 3, 1874 he started a newspaper called the Religious Messenger valued at $18,000 complete with a printing press. The paper was economically sustainable and featured an editorial column he wrote in each publication about the needs of orphan children and widows in Texas after the Civil War. In 1875 he moved the press to Dallas, and in 1876 he changed the name to the Texas Baptist. It was through the Texas Baptist that he raised the vision of the orphan child and convened a Deacon's Convention in Paris in July of 1877 to raise funds for the Buckner Orphan's Home.[15] Buckner served as a pastor, missionary, entrepreneur, publisher, and denominational statesman and at the age of 44, raised a vision to respond to the needs of his day, to shine hope into the world around him. He focused his life on bridging his faith with action. It would take courage, compassion, and conviction to develop redemptive solutions to the lives of people he encountered in Texas at the end of the 19th century.

WHAT KIND OF WORLD DID BUCKNER LIVE IN?

Dr. Karen O. Bullock, Buckner historian and professor has helped us gain an appreciation for the kind of world Robert Cooke Buckner lived in. [16] He was born within a generation of the Revolutionary War period and the first Constitution, and just 30 years after the Louisiana Purchase of 1803, which expanded U.S. territory to an area that now encompasses 15 states. About the same time, Lewis and Clarke's famous Corps of Discovery Expedition of 1805 brought back tales of the vast territory to be explored and fired the imagination of settlers who longed to see the vistas for themselves. In fact, while he was a youth, all of the boundaries of the U.S. locked into place with the annexation of Texas in 1848, the addition of the Great Salt Lake region and the Northwest Territories coalescing into the present nation's landmass (Alaska and Hawaii would come later). Buckner's world was expanding at a time when the nation's greatest builders were at work developing a young country.

BUCKNER'S WORLD WAS BUILDING

RC Buckner was a contemporary of Cornelius Vanderbilt (1794-1877), builder of the Grand Central Railway; Andrew Carnegie (1835-1919) tycoon of the steel industry; JP Morgan (1873-1913), creator of banking and Wall Street; John D. Rockefeller (1839-1937), tycoon of Standard Oil; Henry Ford (1863-1947), who built a car for every home, and Walter Rauschenbusch (1861—1918), Baptist pastor and Father of the Social Gospel movement in the North. He ranks with the builders of our nation. His life was fixed to the God whose call he obeyed.[17] Buckner's world was expanding and was building but it was exploding at the same time.

BUCKNER'S WORLD WAS EXPLODING

He lived through the Mexican War (1846-1848) where his own brother Bennet Burrow, died at 23 years of age in Mexico City, the day after peace was declared in 1848; Buckner was 14 years old. He also saw the horrific scenes of the Civil War (1861-1865) and when he was 30 he saw the scenes of the Spanish-American War (1989) which left women and children and families ravaged by the effects of bloodshed. So many fathers never returned from battle. He lived through not one, but 3 presidential assassinations: President Lincoln (1865) when he was 32 years old; President Garfield (1881) when he was 48; and President McKinley (1901) when he was 68 years old. He was old enough to remember and old enough to feel like his world was crumbling apart.[18] While Buckner's world was exploding with the trauma and pain of the Mexican War, the Civil War, and the assassination of three U.S. presidents, social problems were also growing and suffering was widespread.

BUCKNER'S WORLD WAS SUFFERING

The lack of proper health care struck close to home when a near fatal bout of typhoid pneumonia almost claimed his own life at age 24 in Kentucky. Because of his illness and slow recovery, he and his wife, Vienna Long, packed their two daughters and moved 900 wagon miles to Northeast Texas where they found a warmer climate, arriving in Texas about 1859. In the coming years as he served among Texas Baptists, he saw hundreds of children without homes, elderly people with no means of support, and the dire need for health care, hospitals, and sanitariums to protect the general population from contagious diseases like whooping cough, meningitis, measles, influenza, typhoid, and tuberculosis.[19] The suffering Buckner experienced was not limited to health issues, rather, social issues added to the context of suffering at the turn of the century.

Social injustice and the evils of poverty, hunger, child abandonment, and slavery (children were purchased for servants and field hands, abused and replaced when they died of overwork, starvation, and neglect), racism, and illiteracy were rampant. Laws were not yet written to protect the most vulnerable (Buckner was a part of Child Labor Laws that began in 1904). He saw tuberculosis sweep through the South, including the worldwide influenza epidemic of 1912 and 1918.[20] The things that Buckner believed shaped what he did in response to the conditions he experienced.

WHAT DID BUCKNER BELIEVE?

Dr. Buckner represented Texas Baptists who "believed strongly in a reformed society built upon 'remade men.' These Baptists saw no contradiction between theological conservatism and social activism, and remained unyieldingly committed to the concept of individual salvation as the cure for social inequities."[21] One of the most influential 20th century Baptist leaders and thinkers, Dr. T. B. Maston, agreed with Buckner insisting that the best way to reform society was to "remake the man."[22] Buckner's theology informed his methodology; his beliefs shaped his actions; his faith shaped his works and the kind of leadership he demonstrated during this time in our nation's history.

Buckner and the Texas Baptists that he led saw "no need to shift theologically from the stance of individual regeneration as the key to societal change."[23] In other words, Buckner held that regeneration of the individual was the key to reformation of society; personal evangelism was connected to social objectives. To help us get our arms around this concept, Bullock defines this movement as "Social Christianity" not to be confused with the "Social Gospel," a movement featuring social activism based on a liberal interpretation of scripture.[24] The "Social Gospel" movement was developed by theologians like Walter Rauschenbusch about 50 years after Dr. Buckner began his work.[25] Buckner found his sweet spot between conservative theology and social activism and framed a way of serving that could be called practical Christianity, modeling his efforts after James's idea that "faith without deeds is dead."[26] While he was interested in the social well-being of those he served he was equally passionate about meeting spiritual needs as well. Buckner found his place of work in the zone of redemption by striking a balance between social service and the work of personal regeneration of the heart for every person he served. He saw the redemptive potential of every child and elder that came into his care. He focused his efforts on applying the principles of the gospel to society's ills and demonstrated how to practice Christianity. These core and foundational beliefs drove him to action to transform the society in which he lived. These bed-rock beliefs informed what he did.

WHAT DID BUCKNER DO?

Raising this question opens the floodgates of one life devoted to making a difference as an agent of redemption in the world. Maybe I should have asked: What did he not do? It would be easier to dedicate a few short sentences to that question. And keep in mind that his life's work was accomplished without the use of computers, email, internet, and all the modern technology that makes us more effective. Given the kind of world he lived in and given what he believed, Father Buckner went to work to transform and reform the society in which he lived. He made a difference in the lives of children, African American children especially, the aged, race reconciliation, education, women's theological education, healthcare, prison reform, legal reform, and an array of humanitarian endeavors.

His passion for the well being of children drove him to begin an orphan's home in 1879 starting in his own home before a place was built; he started the Dickson Negro Orphanage in 1885; the Goodnight Academy Home and urged the care for elders and ministers who retired and were destitute. He worked tirelessly for race relations between African American and Anglo leaders; led an interracial church growth network; and started the first black Baptist newspaper called the Baptist Journal in 1878. In the field of education, he founded more schools than orphanages including vocational and technical schools, three high schools, and night schools for newspaper carriers who worked all day, and the Buckner Home School. In the field of healthcare, Buckner began four hospitals, a center for the treatment of epilepsy, helped to form the Baptist Memorial Sanatorium in 1904 which later became Baylor Healthcare System, now called the Baylor Scott & White Hospital System. In the field of justice, he worked with the Texas Prison System and called for reforms in the humane treatment of inmates. He was appointed to the National Conference of Charities and Corrections from 1885 — 1915 and among many other projects in prison reform, he was appointed as a member of the National Prison Association in 1888 and was featured as the keynote speaker in 1899 at the national convention.[27] Throughout all these activities he continued to serve as pastor to the children at the Buckner Orphan's home, preaching weekly among those he served.

In the legal and political field, Buckner was involved in shaping the Texas Child Labor Laws (1902-1916); helped to pass laws protecting mothers and children abandoned by husbands and fathers (1908); and was appointed by President Roosevelt to serve on the White House Conference on Dependent Children; he shaped the Children's Bureau Bill in 1908. In humanitarian work, Buckner founded the Dallas Humane Society in 1888 serving both children and animals; and was instrumental in founding the American Red Cross working alongside Clara Barton in Galveston, Texas following the hurricane disaster of 1900.[28] Father Buckner sought to shape his world through social service, government engagement, business and healthcare innovation, and educational entrepreneurism. He was active helping to shape and reform society by improving and introducing laws at the state and national level; he was active with community and business leaders to build better societies through the humane treatment of children and animals and the embellishment of healthcare institutions; he was active in the educational field by providing educational opportunities and pioneering night school educational environments; and he activated a congregational base of volunteers to engage in practical Christianity.

Robert Cooke Buckner was indeed an agent of redemption, on mission with Jesus to transform his world. Everything he did can be linked back to what he understood to be the teachings of Jesus as recorded in the Bible and specifically reflected in the epistle of James. This moral framework guided the way he saw his world and prompted him to action to reform society so that it better reflected the Kingdom of God on earth. He led through compassion, conviction, and courage.

Another way of summarizing his life's work is by understanding his worldvoice, worldview, and worldvenue. "Worldvoice is the voice of a virtuous person, the paradigmatic person who is the mentor of a culture. Worldview is the mental view of intellectual precepts, the holistic way of perceiving reality that flows from the prototype person. Worldvenue is the manifest venue of social pathways, the social life system of everyday customs and behaviors which flow from the worldvoice person and the worldview precepts. Thus a cultural matrix is recognized by its distinctive dimensions of Wv3: Worldvoice *adoration*, worldview *analysis*; and Worldvenue *avenues*."[29]

In other words, Buckner was guided by the voice of Jesus, the moral prototypical person and mentor as recorded in the Bible. Jesus was his "luminary voice, the person who is looked to for one's life standard. Jesus is the culture's person of excellence who sets the standards of noble conduct for the culture. Jesus is the person whose character traits exemplify the kind of person others in that culture ought to be or to emulate."[30] Buckner perceived reality through a particular lens, viewing and analyzing his world reality through the lenses of the Redeemer of life. Buckner used a "comprehensive vision, and arrangement of analysis." He used a "vital mindset for social creations, produced and sustained by communities of people in order to understand and live in their world" as a paradigm linked back to his luminary, Jesus.[31] Buckner took action and avenues that led to an improved society. He developed a "configuration of social life, the observable and persistent differences in the global cultural zones, the tangible and visible differences between social experiences and behaviors that flow from the particular voice and vision of society.[32] His luminary shaped his lens, and his lens led to a particular lifestyle that made a redemptive and transformational impact in his world.

A clear and simple review of his life's work would lead any reasonable person to conclude Buckner left a large footprint and fingerprint on the City of Dallas, on the state of Texas, and across the United States for decades to come. R. C. Buckner is probably the best model of an agent of redemption in the 20th century in the United States of America and in American Christianity. He serves as a beacon of light and an example of how agents of redemption in the 21st century might live and act. We have Buckner to consider in light of Jesus of Nazareth, our prototype who taught his followers to "do unto others as you would have them do unto you." The teachings of Jesus of Nazareth were at the core of Buckner's ministry. How would we live as agents of redemption with compassion? What are our challenges today to live as agents of redemption full of conviction that mirrors Buckner's view of Social Christianity? How might we live as agents of redemption with the courage to make a difference here in our communities, in our counties, in our country, and in nations abroad?

We might be in a better position to answer these questions as we consider what Buckner currently does globally but what the ministry also does locally. Buckner International has become a global ministry yet its beginning had a very local flavor.

DISCUSSION QUESTIONS

1. James 1:27 caught the imagination of one man who changed Dallas, Texas forever. How does this verse speak to you?

2. An agent of redemption is a person of courage, compassion, and conviction. How do these words describe you?

3. What would be the evidence in your life for The Pattern?

4. How is Dr. R. C. Buckner's world like our world today?

5. What needs attention most in your community?

FIVE:

Redemption in the Local Village

"The King will reply, 'I tell you the truth, whatever you did for one of the least of these brothers of mine, you did for me."

MATTHEW 25:40

"SUPPOSE, BROTHER DEACON, THAT HAD BEEN YOUR CHILD AND YOU DEAD."

An agent of redemption is a person who looks at his or her world wondering how the Kingdom of God can come near in his or her local community in real and tangible ways. That person begins by doing something; by getting involved; and by taking action, redemptive action from his or her circle of influence. This is exactly what Dr. Robert Cooke Buckner did by convening a group of church leaders at a statewide Deacon's convention on July 17, 1877 at the First Baptist Church of Paris, Texas. It was time to take action to serve the "least of these," children that had become orphans just after the Civil War.

Just outside the church meeting of the Deacons, Buckner gathered a smaller group of preachers and said, "Just to give it a start" and took out the first greenback and placed it on his knee. B.H. Carroll said "Amen" and put down the second dollar. So at the age of 44, Buckner rallied these preachers to raise $27.86 that they then took into the meeting. By 1879, with $2,000 raised Buckner opened the Buckner Orphan's home in Dallas in a rented house at the corner of Junius and Haskell. John Cruse and Alice Cruse, from McKinney and John Jones from Ellis County were the first three children admitted to the Buckner Orphan's Home.[1] This was Buckner's response to a need in the local village. He took individual responsibility, engaged lay leaders, activated a congregational base of support, and began doing social Christianity.[2]

Dr. Buckner often posed a question in his message to church leaders whenever he spoke about the conditions of orphan children in Texas after the Civil War saying, "Suppose, Brother Deacon, that had been your child and you dead." The people of Texas responded by sending dry goods, donated cows, boars and sows, turkey eggs, and lumber. They sent their pennies, stitched quilts, canned jars of vegetables, and raised wheat for Father Buckner's children.[3] Buckner applied the Golden Rule to ministry among children, saying, "As you would that others should do to your children, if you should die and leave them homeless and dependent, do ye even unto their children under similar circumstances."[4] This message spoke to the heart of people all across Texas and started a movement that has continued for over 136 years. While Buckner International started as Buckner Orphans Home in Dallas, an orphanage for children and safe haven for widows, the ministry has evolved and adapted its approach since 1879 in the local village to provide safe, family environments for children to develop their redemptive potential rather than live in institutional settings that are often detrimental to the development of a child. The ministry has shifted its focus from institutional care to family preservation and child permanency. The ministry has developed a philosophy of care that advances the conviction that the best place for a child to grow up and develop is within a healthy family environment.

Over the past 136 years, the ministry of Buckner in the local village has grown from one campus in Dallas to a state-wide network of Christ-centered social services for "the least of these," vulnerable children, seniors, and their families all across Texas. The ministry, as an agent of redemption, provides a wide array of social services among children and seniors by shining hope through solutions for their lives from the beginning to the ending of life. Buckner focuses on four primary services: Foster Care and Adoption, Family Pathways, Family Hope Centers, and Retirement Communities.

ADOPTION INTO A FOREVER FAMILY

John and Emily Wiggins were 24 years old and newly married when they drove more than 16 hours to a hospital in Dallas. Four-year-old Juan Pablo had been flown in from Guatemala with then Buckner director Chiqui de Mollinedo and her husband, Sergio, a doctor. They were meeting with a team of doctors to inquire about a series of nodules on Juan Pablo's neck. Mollinedo knew the couple wanted to adopt Juan Pablo, whom they had only met one time, but she also wanted them to have realistic expectations. She asked John and Emily if they would still continue the adoption process if the diagnosis was a terminal illness.

Regardless of the outcome, the Wiggins knew that God had called them to Juan Pablo, and he would lead them through that journey. "Looking back now, it all seems kind of crazy," John said. "We had been married less than two years when we came to Dallas. We were making a big decision for our family. But we felt like God led us to Juan Pablo." Emily remembers sitting in the waiting room with her husband and friends from Buckner, praying for good results when the doctors came out. "They were crying," she said, "and they told us it wasn't cancer. We just totally laid ourselves out there. It's really a miracle how everything has worked out and to see how God has taken care of Juan Pablo through the process."

Juan Pablo was a favorite child of many short-term mission volunteers to Guatemala. He had an infectious smile and a tender heart; he often cared for the younger children like a big brother at the Buckner Baby Home in Guatemala City. But Juan Pablo was different from the other children. At three months old, he was badly burned in a gas explosion along with his mother. They were brought to a hospital where Juan Pablo would live the next six months of his life. Once he recovered, he was placed in a government orphanage, but his face would never be the same. While his mother also recovered from this injury, she abandoned Juan Pablo because she could not care adequately for him.

In 2006, Buckner opened a group home for babies and toddlers in Guatemala City, and Juan Pablo was one of the first children to live there. Since Mollinedo's husband was a doctor, Buckner typically accepted children with severe medical needs in order to provide them with the best care possible. The teal-colored home became a regular stop for mission teams to Guatemala, where volunteers would hold the babies and play games with the toddlers. The Wiggins first spent time with Juan Pablo at this home. "We went on a Shoes for Orphan Souls mission trip in 2005 with Moody Radio and then got our church in Terre Haute, Indiana involved to go on another trip in 2006," Emily said. "We played with him on that trip, but adoption never even crossed my mind."

Later, the couple started to think about adoption and called Buckner to learn more about their options. At the time, Buckner was only placing toddlers into adoptive families and the Wiggins originally wanted a baby. "Our pastor wrote a story about Juan Pablo after a trip, talking about when he looked at JP, he didn't see scars, but only beauty just as Jesus sees him. We didn't feel at peace about adopting a baby and we started praying about it, asking, 'Who would Jesus choose?'" It was this prayer that led the Wiggins to Dallas in September 2007 to spend a week with Juan Pablo, visiting doctors and trusting God with their family's future. Anyra Cano, Buckner adoption caseworker for Guatemala, said the Wiggins felt a deep calling to adopt Juan Pablo. "We told them that adoptions were closing in Guatemala in a few months, and they knew there were risks involved. But they remained faithful. They always said they would keep going until God closes all the doors."

Inter-country adoptions from Guatemala underwent a firestorm of criticism in 2006 when allegations of lawyers coercing birth mothers to sell their children caused the country to close its adoption program. All adoptions initiated prior to December 2007 were "grandfathered" in, but the process was unpredictable. The Wiggins started their adoption just a few months before this final deadline. "While on one of their many trips to Guatemala and the embassy, they were told that the adoption couldn't continue because they were missing one document," Cano said. After a week of prayers and trips to the Embassy, the paperwork finally came through.

"It was a miracle," Cano said. This was just one example of the numerous roadblocks and victories celebrated throughout their three-year journey. In total, the Wiggins would make 10 trips to Guatemala to see Juan Pablo and spend time with the other children at the Buckner group home while the adoption paperwork was under way. "They were faithful to all the children, not just to Juan Pablo," Cano said. "They would do special things for the children, take them on field trips or dress up as superheroes. They wanted all the children to experience the same things Juan Pablo did."

John said the adoption process helped strengthen their marriage as they learned to trust God and rely on one another through the hard times. "We were married a little over a year when we started the adoption process. Our marriage *is* Juan Pablo," he said. Cano said the couple grieved through the setbacks along the way, "but it was never too hard for them to give up. They loved Juan Pablo and knew God intended him to be with their family forever." In November of 2009, the Wiggins went to Guatemala for the last time. Emily was five-months pregnant. "It was a good bonding experience for us," Emily said, remembering the month they spent with Juan Pablo in Guatemala while waiting for the last paperwork to come through. "At that time, he knew we were his parents. He would keep coming up to us and saying, 'My family', kissing and hugging us," she said.

Everyone at the government office in Guatemala was impressed with their journey.

One Guatemalan caseworker said she was "taken aback that such a young family would do so much for a child most other families would not even consider," Cano said. "They made an impression on a lot of people." On December 9, 2009, Juan Pablo came home. He was greeted first in Dallas by Buckner staff and friends, and then welcomed in Indiana by an airport lobby filled with church members, friends, and family. "I had been looking forward so long to having a son, to hear him call me 'Papa,'" John said. "It still sends tingles down my spine."

Juan Pablo has made a big impact on their local community, too. After years of support from their church family, John said it's good for the kids at church to see that "God answers prayers. He had a plan for Juan Pablo's life and now he's part of their life." There have been some challenges for Juan Pablo, and for his parents, since he came home, Emily said. Sometimes children point and stare at him when they're walking in the park because they've never seen someone with burns on their face. She and John have been working with Juan Pablo to help him deal with his feelings. God has also been teaching them how to deal with other people in these situations. "Our prayer is that someday JP will be able to respond with confidence all that God has brought him through and done in his life," Emily said

Juan Pablo came back to Texas in October 2010, one year after their plane touched down. This time, he was counting in English and looking after his baby brother Sam. The Wiggins brought with them several bags filled with new shoes for Buckner's Shoes for Orphan Souls project, collected by their Vacation Bible School at church. "Will Danny and Estuardo be getting new shoes?" Juan Pablo asked when they arrived. He was still thinking about his friends in Guatemala. "Juan Pablo is different from other kids because of the care and love he received at Buckner," Emily said. "Once people get to know him, they realize he's a friend for life," John said.

Cano said the Wiggins have made a commitment to keep Guatemala, Juan Pablo's friends and his heritage as part of their family. They are already planning a return trip to see everyone again, though many of his friends now live in different group homes and foster families. "The Wiggins are a great testimony to what faithfulness and selflessness really mean," she said. They understand what Jesus meant when he said, "I tell you the truth, whatever you did for one of the least of these brothers of mine, you did for me." Foster Care is another way to serve the least of these. The Wiggins, agents of redemption, are instruments of God's grace and love for JP, forever.

I remember Juan Pablo from some of the very earliest trips I made to Guatemala. He was always so cheerful and loving. He impressed me as having an overcoming spirit. To see him today as part of the Wiggins family warms my heart all over again. He has a forever family who loves him and a bright future because of these agents of redemption.

FOSTER CARE TO FAMILY PHOTO

As her family shuffled around, arranging themselves for the perfect family portrait in a Sears studio, Crystal Press stood off to the side with her head down. Her mother Alicia called out for her to join her parents and three siblings in front of the camera. Crystal, 17, quietly walked over, sat for one photo and immediately went back to her previous position behind the photographer. A single tear slipped from her chocolate brown eye and slid down her cheek. Alicia saw the tear. She carefully approached her newly adopted daughter. "Crys, what's wrong?" she asked. Crystal remained silent for a few minutes until she could muster up an answer. "It's just … I've never been allowed in a family picture before."

But being shuffled between foster homes for years, Crystal was often asked to stand aside while her foster families took Christmas card photos to send out to relatives. The Presses were the sixth family who said they would adopt her. They decided to get professional family pictures taken to commemorate Crystal's first day as their foster daughter. She knew she was going to have to learn what it meant to be a part of a real family.

Alicia Press, 28, was adopted by her mother's husband when she was 14, both of whom gave her a happy home and stirred her interest in adoption. She and her husband Tyler Press, 29, both felt called to adopt children for a long time before they decided to become foster-to-adopt parents through Buckner Children and Family Services. Both worked with children in their professions — Alicia as an elementary school principal and Tyler as a youth pastor — and saw firsthand the effects of bad home situations. "We saw it every single day, these kids without good homes," said Tyler, who is now a young adult pastor. "When you can change the life of a child and give them a good home … How could we not?"

Tyler and Alicia spent a year praying about becoming foster parents after gathering all the information from Buckner. They knew it was not going to be an easy road, and still wanting a birth child, they were unsure what the Lord wanted them to do. They thought they would become foster-to-adopt parents, adopt one child, have one of their own and be done. But that was not what God had in store. Within the first three months of being certified in August 2009, the Presses took in three children under the age of three, one of whom was five days old with severe medical issues. The day after they picked up their five-day-old foster son from the hospital, Alicia found out she was pregnant.

The Presses had a feeling they would end up adopting from the youth group at their church but always believed it would be the child of one of the teens with an unplanned pregnancy. Tyler met Crystal as a 13-year-old while he was her youth pastor at church in 2008. Alicia recalls a night at church camp with Crystal that set the tone for the next three years. "We were all in our beds and she jumped in mine, and we giggled and talked about boys and stuff," Alicia said. "But then all of a sudden, the conversation turned serious. She talked about this great desire she had for a family. We just prayed and prayed and prayed that God would give her a real family. It was one of those crying, snot-everywhere kind of things, but I had no idea what was coming next."

After being shuffled between foster homes and finally landing in a group home, Crystal learned the group home would be closing and she had nowhere to go. When the Presses heard the news, they felt a tugging on their hearts. They cared about Crystal a lot, but there were a lot of factors that made the situation seem impossible, namely the age difference. Crystal was only 11 years younger than the Presses. "We just had no idea," Alicia said. "We prayed on our hands and knees forever. I just said, 'Lord, what do you want from me? I'm 27. She's 16.'"

In November 2010, Crystal moved in as their foster daughter. Her adoption was finalized five months later. "We know it's different," Tyler said. "When people see her run up to me and give me a hug, they think it's weird. But we don't feel the need to explain it to anyone." Adjusting to permanent family life hasn't been easy, but the Presses never give up on Crystal. "She's a teenager, and she acts like one," Tyler said, laughing.

"But we always tell her that no matter how much trouble she gets in, we love her. We'll always love her." "Crystal has shown me things about life I never had learned," Alicia added. "She is just such an amazing, neat person. She's made a commitment to put the past behind her. She's learning the right thing to do."

The Presses have had five foster children since they were certified, and have adopted Crystal and Emily, a five-year-old spitfire who loves goofing around and playing soccer. They finalized their adoption of Jayden, 3, in December 2011. Their birth son, Pierceton, 2, loves chasing after his older brother. Crystal is thriving as a sophomore in high school. She's the editor of her school yearbook. She loves playing with her younger siblings, although she admits, like most teenagers, that they drive her a little crazy sometimes. "I just thought about what my life would have been like if I hadn't been adopted. I have the utmost respect for my (adoptive) dad. He is a wonderful man," Alicia said. "I wanted to give that to someone else." The Presses have put foster care on hold but continue to serve as advocates in their community for Buckner and for foster care. "They're walking with Christ, and they're so grateful to take in children who need them," Buckner Midland case manager Sarah Hataway said. "They put themselves aside and they're doing it for the right reasons."

When I first heard of Crystal's story, I choked up and fought back the tears. I was home reading and writing when I read her story. I had to take a break. Crystal's story touched my heart and brought me to tears. I had to get up, leave my office, and take a break. I went to the kitchen to get something to drink and on the way to the kitchen I walked passed all our Christmas photographs and family photos over 33 years of marriage. I remember thinking that there was never a question about who would be in the photo. Crystal's story impacted me even more. I thought "this is not right." I came away even more committed to find families for children who could be included in a Christmas photo and know that this is where they belong. The Press family is an instrument in the hands of God to help Crystal become all that God has intended for her in her future. They are agents of redemption.

Crystal's life is being redeemed. All that was intended to harm her is being turned into good, thanks to the Press family and their willingness to make room for one more family member in their family photo. Sometimes our ministry is about building families to find permanent solutions for children but sometimes our ministry is about protecting and preserving families that are currently struggling; surviving from abuse, abandonment, and neglect; carving out a pathway to a healthy environment and future filled with hope.

A FAMILY PATHWAY FOR AMBER'S FAMILY

With her two small children in tow, a bruised face and a heavy heart, 20-year-old Amber Fowler packed up her few belongings and headed into the snow-covered streets of a frigid Washington winter, unsure of where to go. She was 2,000 miles away from her family and home in Texas. She and her children's father had another big fight and, this time, enough was enough. Amber found a local shelter and was placed in a transitional housing program. She got a house, found a job and enrolled in school. She was convinced things were going to be different. But then she let her boyfriend back into her life and, soon after, she was pregnant with her third child, Fred, now 5. And it all fell apart again.

Amber is now a 26-year-old single mother with four children, ages 10, 6, 5 and 3. She dropped out of school and left home against her father's urging at the age of 13 and spent the next several years living on the streets, in shelters and in sub-standard housing. She suffered multiple failed relationships, plagued by domestic violence, drug and alcohol abuse and unplanned pregnancies. She had her first daughter, Frankie, at age 15. She and Frankie's father lived together off and on but eventually she decided to leave because she knew life could be different. She was 17 when she left. She went to another shelter for a couple of weeks and managed to get her own apartment and a job. Amber didn't seem to have too much trouble finding jobs, but she never made enough money to support herself, let alone a family. Without a high school education, employment was limited.

In 2005, she "made a bad decision and ended up on the streets again," she said. The two went to another shelter, which is where she met her youngest kids' dad. They got jobs and an apartment, and got back on their feet. Amber got pregnant with her second daughter, Rebecca, now 6. They decided to move to Washington with his family. "I'd never been out of Texas and we were in love," Amber recalled. "His mom was up there and she had a job for him and a car for us to drive. We had a whole little house to ourselves. So I said, 'Cool, let's go.' I only had two kids at the time." The situation quickly escalated into a nightmare, she said. Her girls witnessed a lot of the chaos. She tried to escape, but they always got back together.

Amber became pregnant with Fred before deciding to return home to her family. In 2008, they came back to Texas and Rachel, her last child, was born in 2010. Amber managed to get away from her children's father and get her own apartment in Conroe, still working dead-end jobs, still wanting to go to school, still fighting to make ends meet. But she didn't feel safe and felt like she still needed to get away from her children's father so once again, they headed to a shelter. But this time, the outcome was different. Amber met Brenda Shuttlesworth, then program director of Buckner Family Place in Conroe. After hearing about Family Place — a self-sufficiency program that provides housing and supportive services for single-parent families while parents pursue their education full-time — she quickly applied and was accepted.

"When I met Amber, I knew she was just one of those people who had a lot of potential if she were ever given a break in life," Shuttlesworth said. "She's very bright. And Amber truly knows the world. She knows what it's like to struggle, yet through education, she's going to have a better life for herself and for her children." Amber is a survivor and wants people to know that the hope that shines forth in her life comes from her personal relationship with Jesus Christ. Since coming to Buckner, Amber has taken parenting classes, abuse recovery classes and most importantly, earned her GED and enrolled in college. School hasn't come without its challenges, especially while trying to keep track of four children, but somehow, she manages. "I couldn't do it without God. He is my rock and to Him all the glory, truly," she said. "But we have a routine that we stick to and it normally all goes smoothly. I look at it like my own little assembly line."

Amber gets to school by 8 a.m. to do homework for two hours before her first class. She has a three-and-a-half hour class, a 20-minute break for more homework and then another three-hour class. She stays at school until 6 p.m. to do homework and then heads home to get her four kids to start on their evening routine. The kids are more secure in their physical location and also in their family relationship. Each child gets to spend one-on-one time with their mom. Sometimes they go ice skating or get their nails done. They have play dates with their cousins, go to the movies, go to the zoo, and have birthday parties. A non-negotiable for each of her kids is a college education. "If there's one thing I hope my kids have learned through all this, it's to go to college and to know that I would never leave them. They're not going to decide to drop out of school; they're not going to get pregnant. They're not going to do the things I did. They are going to college."

Amber acknowledges that she's changed a lot since coming to Family Place and that she has a long way to go. She's more secure with herself and doesn't second-guess everything like she used to. She's learning to process how she was raised and how to change her future. She frequently has to ask for help at school because she doesn't have the educational foundation from junior high and high school, but the teachers who know her story are supportive. She struggles with math but she placed into college-level English when she took the entrance exam for Lone Star State College.

She received her associate's degree in the spring of 2013 and hopes to obtain her bachelor's degree and then continue on to seminary to become a social worker. "I feel like shelters are going to be part of my ministry," Amber said. "I want to help families and children, mostly mothers, to be able to provide for the children in a sufficient way, kind of like Buckner is doing for us. I've been in situations where I know that my experience can help other women. I want to let them know that regardless of where you come from, there's hope — and anyone can make it."

Amber wants to work for Child Protective Services as a social worker but she doesn't want to stop there. She wants to help make changes and raise money for CPS organizations.

Sometimes, when she reflects on her life, she doesn't even recognize who she used to be, she said. "I've experienced a lot," Amber said. "But when I'm sitting here, talking about it, it's like a whole other person. Even when I think about how others view me, I just think there's no way I'm that person. I'm not sure how I ever was that person. But God has shown himself true in my life." Amber is taking parenting classes and also completed abuse recovery at a local church. She's interested in other self-help classes the church offers because she likes the Biblical basis for the lessons. Shuttlesworth has seen the changes in Amber, too. Her communication style is different, both with her children and her peers. She's not as prone to raise her voice. She places more value on education and helping herself. She is slowly learning to trust people again.

The first Family Place residents in Conroe began the program in 2010. The program is a community-based model that includes a lot of small group meetings between the mothers. Their groups are spiritually based, depending on what's going on in everyone's lives. Shuttlesworth believes the community aspect is what leads to success in the program. "Another reason why I wanted Buckner so bad was because I wanted to be different," Amber said." Amber wanted to live a different life than her family had when she was young. She wanted to be a different parent to her children than her mom was to her. The holistic aspect is really what enticed her. She said, "the part where it teaches us to become self-sufficient and to be OK in our own skin, and to trust our judgment. It's taught me so much. And I am truly grateful and humbled to be in the program." Reflecting on her experience, Amber said, "No matter how far gone, messed up or worthless you feel you are, there is always hope. Faith in Jesus Christ is the only thing that has truly gotten me this far. Always have faith in your abilities and the love or God, and you should be fine. There is always a way out. I have found, by searching, that God is the only way for me and my family." Amber found a new pathway to hope, a new pathway to the future for her family. Her life and the lives of her children are being redeemed.

Amber's story is an example of what Buckner is doing in communities all over Texas with moms who just need an opportunity to be affirmed, loved, and encouraged to find a new path for success. The core factor that leads to success for these moms and their families is the opportunity to anchor their lives with faith commitments. Moms like Amber have an opportunity to experience the unconditional love of Jesus from staff members who serve as agents of redemption. Buckner ministry provides opportunities to find a permanent solution for a child through adoption and sometimes through Foster Care. On many occasions we have the privilege of preserving families like Amber's. Another way we build strong families is by serving them before they fall apart.

STRENGTHENING FAMILIES AT FAMILY HOPE CENTERS

Seven brides take turns posing one at a time beneath a red and white ribbon-bedecked arch at the end of the sanctuary's center aisle. One of the husbands-to-be snaps photos with his tablet next to the wedding photographer. You can see some of the pre-wedding jitters begin to melt away as the women laugh and loosen up during portraits. A storm rolls in and the air smells like rain. One of the brides, late to her own wedding, nearly gets caught in the downpour. Her hair is slightly dampened, but her spirits are not; she's looked forward to this day for a long time. This wedding is in no way typical. There are seven couples of all ages and all different stories, all waiting to be married on the same night. The youngest bride is 16 and eight months pregnant. The oldest is in her mid-40s.

These diverse families have been brought together by their connection to the Buckner Family Hope Center in Peñitas, Texas. They have all reached a point of newfound confidence in their lives and relationships — a confidence that's allowing them to finally tie the knot. "One of the things I'm so excited about today is that I see the hope in these families," says Ricardo Brambila, director of the Family Hope Center and officiate for the wedding ceremony. "Their children are so excited because they're going to see mom and dad getting married. It began with the conversation we had with them in the family strengthening class — how are you going to tell your kids to get married someday if you're not married?"

All seven couples are in case coordination at the Hope Center, Brambila says, and all have been together for anywhere from three to 12 years. "For them, the Hispanic culture is that they think, 'We might not make it,'" Brambila says. "They don't want to commit because they don't know if they're going to make it, because first they need to meet their needs. But once their basic needs are met and they're stronger as a family, they begin thinking about morals. It's like a threshold. Once your basic needs are met, you begin to think through the future." While Brambila briefs the couples on the order of service, family and friends visit and find seats. Little boys in clean, pressed button-down shirts and slick, combed hair sink into the pews with bored looks on their faces. Girls in sequined dresses and bows giggle as they run through the church in small packs.

Four couples have opted for a religious ceremony and three chose a civil ceremony. The stormy weather has Judge Jesse Contreras, officiate for the civil ceremony, running late, but the religious ceremony is scheduled to start first, anyway. Brambila opens with a greeting and prayer and gives the stage to Pastor Fidencio Vasquez of Primera Iglesia Bautista La Joya, who gives a brief sermon about the gravity of the vows the couples are about to make. "Marriage isn't for a week," he says. "Marriage isn't for a month. Marriage isn't for a year. When bad things happen in life, you must take advantage of the opportunity to learn and to form stronger relationships in marriage." Ten minutes in, the youngest children lose interest and are shushed by Brambila several times throughout the service. Older kids are milling around, taking photos of their parents' big moment. The wedding incorporates traditional Hispanic rites rich in symbolism and culture.

Brambila leads the couples through the lighting of unity candles to symbolize their oneness. Next, the godparents of the *lazo* drape a figure-eight shaped rope over the shoulders of each bride and groom, symbolizing the union and love of the couple with each other and with God. The godparents of the *arras* hand each groom 13 gold coins. The groom pours these coins into his brides' cupped hands, symbolizing his role as provider and reassuring his bride that she will never lack anything. Buckner serves as the godparent of Bibles. Each couple receives a copy, and Brambila exhorts the couples to read the Word of God, live it and practice it each day. Adults, teens, and children crowd the stage with cameras, phones and tablets when it's time for exchanging rings and vows. The children are visibly thrilled to see and hear their parents pledge to stay together "for better or worse, for richer or poorer, in sickness and in health, to love and to cherish until death" parts them. With a final prayer, Brambila declares each couple "man and wife."

Judge Contreras takes the stage to perform the nonreligious ceremony for the remaining three couples, but his faith compels him to give a mini-sermon anyway. He talks about how spousal abuse is a problem in the community and tells the men to mimic "the greatest love story ever told" — God's sacrifice of His only Son. He admonishes the grooms to follow the example of Christ in how they treat their wives: to respect them, love them, and sacrifice themselves for their families.

Myrthala Arjona and Julio Cesar Rodríguez Mendoza are one of older couples of the group, and like many of the other couples, their children spurred them to get married. Paula and Paola are twin sisters from Myrthala's previous relationship. The 15-year-olds have been a part of the Family Hope Center's Youth Leaders Program, and Myrthala says she's seen a change in her daughters because of it. "Since joining the Youth Leaders, my daughters have become more helpful to others and concerned about other people and less self-centered," she says. "I'm happy because my kids are always safe there and looked after. I have peace of mind knowing they're in a safe place." The Youth Leaders Program has become part of the Rio Grande Valley Teen Pregnancy Prevention Coalition and has a strong abstinence program, Brambila says.

"We're talking to them about marriage, talking to them about staying pure," Brambila says. "So we're telling the kids these things, and when they go home, the kids say, 'Hey, they talk about marriage — why haven't you two been married?' So when a 14-year-old kid is asking his parents, 'Why haven't you two gotten married?' it starts conversations." Myrthala and Julio Cesar have been together for eight years. They have a great relationship built on good communication and a willingness to keep the past in the past. "He won my children's hearts first and then won mine," she says. "She attends me and uses her serving actions to show that she loves me," he says. "We are both very united in everything."

They had planned to get married for years, but never managed to take the leap. It took the twins' insisting that their parents get married so the family would have God's blessing. It worked. Myrthala looked beautiful on her wedding day in a floor-length silvery-white dress with elaborate embroidery. She found it at the local flea market for just $3. "We didn't have the money to buy something very expensive," she explains. Julio Cesar wore a white suit with coordinating embroidery on the shoulders. They were a perfect pair. The family has found support from the Family Hope Center in other small, but significant, ways. The couple works together picking crops; the girls help out in the summer months. Besides being backbreaking labor (especially in watermelon season), the heat is scorching and the vines rough up their hands. Buckner staff gave each member four sets of work gloves for protection and four hydration packs so they don't have to travel the usual half-mile to the water truck.

"When Becci Ruiz, Buckner case manager, came with the gloves and backpacks, we were thankful and happy," Myrthala says. "It's a small thing, but it makes such a big difference. We're thankful Buckner is here and thankful they're concerned about our family." Myrthala recently began taking computer classes at the center when she's not working. She says her children's schools are switching to digital report cards soon, and the only thing she knows about using a computer is how to turn it on. She says she also wants to be able to monitor what the kids are doing online, and the Family Hope Center is the only place nearby that offers free classes. The family has also received financial assistance from the Center at times, and through the Youth Leaders Program, the girls attend church and come home sharing what they've learned with their parents.

"What we do at the Family Hope Center involves a lot of stuff about God," Paola says. "It's a good influence. Before I started becoming a part of the Youth Leaders, I didn't go to church. I would be misbehaving or talking back. Now, I'm more calm." Brambila said that the Family Hope Center seeks to minister to each family member "because it's not enough to only speak to the needs of the parents or children. For true transformation to occur, we must minister to the needs of all." The stories of these couples getting married strike me as a ray of hope shining into the lives of the children of these families. As a child, what greater confidence might one gain than knowing his or her parents have made a commitment to each other for life? The idea of marriage grew out of self-determined goals set by the couples involved in case coordination at the Family Hope Center. This is one way Buckner strengthens and preserves families. The ministry serves young families but also serve families during the golden years.

Reaching out to families through Family Hope Centers to strengthen them before they disintegrate, preserves families and helps them move from dependence to independence. Through intensive case management, case managers work with families like the Mendozas to plug the holes that keep them from gaining economic strength and family health. While we are not usually in the business of doing weddings, I cannot imagine a deeper investment in the life of a family than for the parents to make life-long commitments to each other for stability, safety, and security for the children in that family. Buckner leaders like Ricardo Brambila and Becci Ruiz are agents of redemption working with children, teens, and families to strengthen and preserve families.

DISCUSSION QUESTIONS

1. In Matthew 25:40, Jesus points to "the least of these" as those worthy of our attention and care. Who are the "least of these" in your circle of influence?

2. If the Kingdom came near to your neighborhood, to your community, what would it look like? What would have to change?

3. What are some practical ways you can serve "the least of these" in your community?

4. How would you want for people to care for your children if you were suddenly absent from their lives?

5. What would it take for you to make room at your table for a child that needs a family?

SIX:

Redemption in the Global Village

"Do not deprive the alien or the fatherless of justice, or take the cloak of the widow as a pledge. Remember that you were slaves in Egypt and the Lord your God redeemed you from there. That is why I command you to do this."

DEUTERONOMY 24:17

"MUCH OF THE BIBLE IS WRITTEN FOR A POOR WORLD AND A POOR CHURCH."

Dr. Phillip Jenkins, Distinguished Professor of History and Co-Director for the Program on Historical Studies of Religion, Institute for Studies of Religion at Baylor University, has written and lectured on the future of Christianity being positioned in the global south: Latin America, Africa, and Asia by 2050. He has said, "much of the Bible is written for a poor world and a poor church."[1] We saw evidence of global poverty with the number of unaccompanied and undocumented minors coming to the U.S. border in 2014 swell to 60,000, almost twice the number of those that come annually. Most of the children came from Guatemala, Honduras, El Salvador, and Mexico. A deeper probe of the reasons for this exodus to the USA by children as young as five years of age revealed poverty, and gang violence as the main reasons for children, teens, and some adults fleeing for their lives.[2] I spoke to Mr. Oscar Padilla, Vice Minister of External Affairs for the Guatemalan government. He mentioned that one mother said, "I would rather my child die on his way to America than die on the front steps of my home due to gang violence." The desperate cry for survival and the daily threat of violence is a reality many children and families face on a daily basis.

This definition of poverty may pose a challenge for North American Christians living in an era of relative prosperity as compared to the rest of the world. How does an agent of redemption reconcile the reality of life in the West with life in the developing world when it comes to matters of faith and action? The advent of the internet, the ease of international travel, the abundance of financial resources, and the opportunity for incarnational presence places heavier responsibility on those of us in the West to serve "the least of these" in our global village. The "least of these" are the groups of people Jesus referred to in Matthew 25:31-46 in his parable about the sheep and goats. In this parable, Jesus says when we give food to the hungry, water to the thirsty, housing for the stranger, clothing to the naked, healing to the sick, and visitation to the prisoner, we also serve him. Jesus said these are "the least of these, his brothers."

An agent of redemption is a person that keeps the memory of his or her redemption constantly in mind. This kind of person is also concerned about the story of redemption beyond the borders of the United States of America, throughout the global village. The vision for ministry among the fatherless has its roots in the teachings of Moses as instructions to the people of Israel before they crossed into the Promised Land. The context of the teaching of Moses brings to light relevant issues regarding the treatment of marginalized and hurting people into sharp focus.

The word, Deuteronomy, means Second Law. Old Testament scholars call it "the Book of Teaching." In fact, it is a book of speeches, sermons, and discourses of Moses in the last few weeks of his life and looks toward Israel's life in the promised land. While it is a book of laws, it plays a major role in the development of Jewish theology and goes beyond the subject to point to religious and ethical implications and appeals to faith and obedience. His audience represents the next generation poised to move into the land they learned about as children, as the next generation prepares to cross into prosperity and blessing.

Now, if you were Moses and you came to the end of your life with one more opportunity to provide wisdom and teaching through your last words, what would you say? What laws would you highlight? What would be salient to a people about to enter into a land flowing with milk and honey? Moses chose to set themes of slavery and prosperity in stark contrast of each other to frame his final instructions to the people of Israel as they prepared to cross over into the promised land.

SLAVERY

This picture may be hard to visualize in our mind's eye primarily because most of us have no idea what slavery means from a personal perspective. Most of us have not had the experience of being owned by another human being. We have not experienced what it feels like to be treated like we were less than human. We may not know what it is like to serve the needs of another every waking moment of every day of our lives under harsh treatment, brutality, and abuse. For Americans, slavery is a distant memory. For the children of Israel, it was a recent memory. They had just escaped from slavery by the mighty hand of the Lord. They were still poor, full of anticipation of reaching the Promised Land and its promised blessings which would allow them to turn their backs to poverty. But would these redeemed slaves be able to remember their roots once in the Promised Land?

PROSPERITY

Prosperity is not so much a stranger. Most of us are familiar with prosperity or what we might call the Promised Land. The Promised Land was a place where the children of slaves were going to be free. Free to pursue their dreams, their hopes, and their aspirations. The Promised Land was a place where there would be plenty to eat, a place full of opportunity to work, to start a family, to enjoy life. Our nation, with all its faults and shortcomings, is sort of that kind of place. We live in the land where many people have the opportunity to pursue a dream, a vision, start a family, enjoy work, and prosperity. We live in the land of three or more meals a day. We live in contrast to those who live on less than a dollar a day for survival. So Moses' words to those living in the land of plenty may actually be a good word to those of us who have lived a life of privilege. Moses may not have known there would be over 200 million orphans in the world but the Lord of Redemption did. Moses may not have known that undocumented immigration and global migration would be an issue in our country, but the Lord of Redemption knew.

What is God's heart for the fatherless in the global village? Moses gives us a bird's eye view to the heart of God for the fatherless, the alien, and the widow in the instructions he leaves for the next generation poised to enter into the Promised Land. The 24th Chapter of Deuteronomy records Moses' instructions from his last words regarding the fatherless, the widow, and the alien. He issues a call to justice, a call to generosity, and a call to redemption as a reflection of God's concern to not exploit those in difficult economic circumstances and to protect the poor, the fatherless, and the widow. Above all, Moses wanted to remind the next generation about their history and their future. He hoped they would not treat people in similar circumstances in life the way they were treated when they were slaves. He wanted them to provide justice for the fatherless, the widow, and the alien. He hoped those in difficult economic circumstances would be treated with generosity and be given opportunity and access to economic independence. He hoped the theme of redemption would not leave their memories when they became landowners, wealthy, and in positions of privilege and power. He wanted to instill in the hearts and minds of the next generation to act in a redemptive way toward those they would encounter in the new land.

What is God's heart for the fatherless in the global village? What should our response be to the 60,000 unaccompanied and undocumented minors that came to our border in 2014 seeking a better life? Some came seeking survival from situations of poverty, gang violence, and drug trafficking. What should our response be to the 151 million orphans in the world who have no family and are trapped in institutional settings or living destitute on the streets subject to human trafficking, sex trade, and other forms of survival? How should we steward our prosperity as we consider the least of these in our global village?

The early 1990s would usher in a new era of redemptive activity for Buckner in the global village to care for the fatherless, the alien, and the widow through issues of justice, generosity, and redemption. Dr. Ken Hall and his wife, Linda, both sensed a call to vocational missions earlier in their ministry but due to circumstances beyond their control, they were not able to pursue this vision. Yet, they kept tucked away deep in their hearts wondering how they might fulfill this calling in their future. The opportunity to live out this vision and to serve the least of these at the same time came when Dr. Hall was elected as the fifth president of Buckner.

INTO THE GLOBAL VILLAGE

Buckner went global in 1994, under the leadership of Dr. Ken Hall, the fifth President and CEO of Buckner. The first destination for Buckner serving orphans was in Russia. Buckner began leading volunteer groups to Russia to work in government-operated orphanages to provide orphan care. Later this ministry led to the beginning of Buckner Adoption and Maternity Services providing licensed inter-country adoption services. This ministry prepared American families to become forever families, families that would be a family for the rest of their lives, for children from Russia. Soon after inter-country adoptions began, Buckner extended placements of children needing homes from Guatemala, Honduras, and Ethiopia. Buckner's experience in inter-country adoption led to opportunities to serve vulnerable children in their own countries beyond inter-country adoption.

Over the last 20 years the organization has expanded services through affiliated non-government organizations in Russia, Mexico, the Dominican Republic, Honduras, Guatemala, Peru, Ethiopia, and Kenya. Early in our international work, the decision was made to hire local indigenous staff that knew the language, culture, and context to help us deliver solutions to vulnerable children and their families in their communities in an expeditious manner. In each country, we made it a point to respond to an invitation from the government to ensure coordination, respect, and support from government officials. Stepping into the global village produced many opportunities to serve the least of these as well as issues of justice, human trafficking, kidnapping, abuse, neglect, and abandonment among children and families in situations unimaginable to most of us.

STOLEN AT BIRTH

Margarita Gomez (her name has been changed to protect her identity) slowly stirs in a dark room. The aches of yesterday's childbirth reverberate through her body. Her hands glide up and down the bed around her, but she doesn't find what she wants. Sitting up, she calls to those who have been taking care of her and ask for her newborn child. You have no child, they respond. It's a lie, Gomez knows, but her life is threatened if she ever professes otherwise. Her baby is gone. Later that day, Gomez and her two young children are loaded onto a bus that returns her to her quiet Guatemalan village. Throughout the next few days, she relives what just happened.

Elvia and Mario Sosa (their names have been changed pending legal action against them) promised to help her. They arranged for a doctor to deliver her child. Yet, shortly after she arrived at their home, she and her children were locked up. The birth of her son was a blur. She never held him; never even saw her boy, Samuel. Now, the Sosas are gone. Three days after the birth of her son, Gomez reports the situation to the police, launching a nationwide search for Samuel. It begins with legal authorities taking Gomez back to Cantel, where she awoke after childbirth. "The only thing I remember is that there was a store right in front of the house. They took me to one street, and it wasn't there. Then to another one and it wasn't there, and so on. I told them that all I remember were some railings on a little hill. That's when we found the house."

Inside the home, they discover the Sosas. And baby Samuel. "They rescued my baby and I saw them when they rescued him," Gomez says. "To be honest, they wouldn't let me see him that day. I was a little upset. I really wanted to meet my baby and I couldn't do it that same day. But I was happy, too, because he was safe and away from the people who stole him from me." Authorities arrested the Sosas and placed Samuel into care at Casa Alegria, a children's center where he would not benefit from "love and care of his mother, brothers and family," said Buckner Guatemala Caseworker Jenifer Montes.

Montes was notified of Gomez's situation by Guatemala's national judicial court. She is part of *Semillas de Esperanza*, a Buckner collaborative effort between Guatemala's child welfare department and Buckner

Guatemala. Her assignment was to perform an investigation and prepare the legal casework necessary to determine whether or not Gomez was the baby's mother. If so, she was to reunite her with her baby.

The *Semillas* project is the outcome of a nearly $1 million grant awarded in 2013 to Buckner by the U.S. Agency for International Development (USAID) to develop programs in Guatemala that will provide permanent family solutions for orphans and vulnerable children. In English, the project is called Fostering Hope Guatemala. In Spanish, the name gets a slight twist: *Semillas de Esperanza* or, literally, "Seeds of Hope."

Carlos Colon, manager of strategic initiatives for Buckner, says the USAID/Guatemala/Buckner collaboration is a "great example of what happens when governmental resources are joined with expertise in child casework. Since Buckner has been active in the Semillas project, we have dramatically increased the number of children who have been taken from dangerous situations and placed into safe care." Among the project's goals are finding ways to locate or provide safe care for children, ages birth through three years, including placing them in foster care or reuniting them with their families. It's a charge that seems to be a perfect fit for cases like Samuel's.

"When I learned it was a kidnapping, a child ripped out of his mother's arms and that she didn't even get to meet him, I felt three times as committed to her and the baby," Montes says. "It seemed so unfair and I felt so powerless. I didn't have the power to fix it immediately." Montes turned to her expertise — and to a higher power — to tackle the case. "When I heard about the case, I asked God to enlighten my mind and to guide me on the right path — which people to talk to, and what it was that he demanded of me for me to be able to serve this family."

The case is the first of its kind for Montes with *Semillas de Esperanza*. Similar cases often lead to dead ends. "In Guatemala, there are hundreds, even thousands of kidnapped children and the mothers — out of fear or because of a threat or ignorance or not knowing what they can do — stay quiet and the children get lost. In irregular adoptions, they get sold.

"In this case, we have to give credit to Margarita," she says. "She was brave and had the courage to come to the authorities and file a report." As Montes works on the case, Gomez fights her own demons while Samuel is in care — and away from her. "I was feeling sad because he wasn't around," she says. "I would cry sometimes, because I didn't have him. When people asked me, I didn't know what to say. I thought I had lost him." Because of the way information is transferred between courts, Montes had to start practically from scratch. As she searched for people and interviewed them, she documented her efforts with law enforcement officials.

"It was really difficult. Since the kidnapping happened in Quetzaltenango, the process got started in a division, a court. And because Margarita lived in another division, the case was transferred, so in that period of time of approximately one month, there was no information about the family, their address or why the child was in custody. During that whole month it was very difficult to get information," Montes said. "Even if we had the address, it is very difficult to go in and walk around. Generally, we had to search for one person at a time and ask them, or store-by-store and ask, 'Do you know Ms. Margarita?' or 'Do you know where she lives? How can I find her?'"

After interviewing Gomez, Montes ordered a DNA test to determine whether she was Samuel's mother. She arranged court hearings for Gomez and Samuel. Seventy-five days after he was placed into state care, a judge granted Gomez provisional care of Samuel. On a cloudless morning in a quiet village, Samuel was finally home with his mother, siblings, uncles and grandmother. Montes smiled at the sight. She helped Gomez fill out the last of the custody forms that signify the end to her long six-month ordeal. When the DNA tests come back positive, Montes says Samuel's "right to have an identity will be restored. Margarita and her children will continue living their lives."

Gomez looks up at Montes with a mother's smile as she hoists baby Samuel into her arms. "I really appreciate [Buckner] a lot because they did a really good job. My baby is with me now. I am very happy." Montes became emotionally invested in the case and said that the joy is mutual. When she found out that Samuel had been reunited with his mother, she "felt a joy that I can't even express with words. It was an overwhelming emotion. I rejoiced. I cried. I must confess that it was very gratifying to know that the effort, the time, the work and everything that gets done coordinating efforts with other institutions and going over to her home to interview her, learning about her story, and having all those little actions add up."

Montes closed the case like she began it: with prayer. "When I found out Samuel had been reunited with his mother, I was just thanking God and glorifying Him for His greatness and mercy, because this is one solved case out of the many kidnapped children. So now, I pray to God to give wisdom to Ms. Margarita."

Sometimes ministry staff and volunteers have the privilege of going into the global village to serve the least of these in other countries and sometimes the least of these of the global village come to our borders.

TRIP TO THE HOME OF THE BRAVE

Daniela Cruz (*Not her real name*) is bone-tired. After a harrowing month on the road from her home in El Salvador, she crossed the Rio Grande River into Texas, was picked up by Border Patrol agents and processed as an undocumented immigrant. She looked forward to a shower — the first she's had in a month — clothing and some food provided at the Catholic Charities Refugee Center at Sacred Heart Catholic Church in McAllen. Among the clothing is shoes collected through Buckner Shoes for Orphan Souls®, available to the waves of children who pass through the center daily with their parents.

The young mother made the journey with daughters Lorena, 8, and Carmen, 6. The decision to go wasn't easy, nor was it inexpensive, but she said it had to be made. "First, it wasn't safe for my children and then there was no employment," she said. "There is nothing you can do in El Salvador now for employment, and I can't even be sure my kids will be safe because of Mara Salvatrucha (a prominent Salvadoran drug gang, also known as MS-13). "One of my nieces was being harassed by the gangs, and I didn't want to have my daughters endure the same treatment." So she and her husband made the decision for her and the girls to travel the dangerous route to the United States to join family in New York. They paid smugglers known as coyotes $3,500 to lead them past her country's border, through Guatemala and Mexico and finally to the U.S. border, where they swam across the Rio Grande.

The family "traveled by bus mainly at night, and stayed in warehouses, sleeping on the floor for 3-5 days at a time while we waited to go from one country to another." Along the way, her daughter became ill, but the family did not have access to medical attention. The coyotes on the Salvadoran side were not nice people. The Cruz family was issued a court date for an immigration hearing in New York. She is planning to attend and waits for her husband, who is planning to make the journey soon.

Javier Perez, manager of missions and humanitarian aid for Buckner International in the Rio Grande Valley, said the Cruzes are among a surge of refugee families that has crossed the border recently in the area. "The people are coming from Mexico, Honduras, Guatemala, and other Central American countries," he said. "Many of them have paid thousands of dollars to coyotes to have them guided here. Most haven't had baths in a while, so they throw their clothes away when they come to the refugee center here. The children's shoes are hanging off their feet because they have walked so much. That's why the shoes are so important."

Buckner shipped 8,000 extra pairs of shoes to the Texas Valley to help in the relief effort. Matt Asato, Buckner senior director of ministry engagement, said the ministry's hope "is that shoes provide the hope and love of Jesus to them. By meeting their physical needs, we hope they will feel that love, despite any political situation. That they will know that people will serve them for who they are: children of God." The Cruz girls were each fitted with a brand new pair of sneakers. Taking advantage of a lull in the line, volunteer Chad Mason, pastor of mobilization and global impact for Calvary Baptist Church in McAllen, let Lorena pick out a favorite pair before placing them on her feet. "Calvary has been working with the refugee center since the third day it went into operation here." he said. "We've been providing volunteers, about 10 per day at the center and an additional 10 doing laundry." The Cruz family is typical of many being served at the center. "These families are typically one mother and two or three small children," Mason said. "The families take an average of 10-12 days on their journey here, plus three to four days in processing by Border Patrol. So by the time they get here, they haven't had a shower or time to themselves or any rest. We've had stories (of trips) that went up to 40 days."

He said the center and its volunteers "first try to give them dignity. So a shower does a lot for someone, plus two or three changes of clothes they can take with them on the bus. These kids getting shoes means everything. This will be a huge blessing for them." Nancy Wagner, a Catholic Charities volunteer from the Diocese of Camden, N.J., echoed that message. "It (shoes) is a desperately needed commodity for them," she said. "Many of them come in with their feet hurting. They've been walking, their shoes are muddy, they're torn and their shoelaces have been taken away by whatever government entity was holding them. This is a really big blessing to have these shoes to give them."

Like many of the volunteers who have given aid to the families at the center, Wagner said she prays "that they find hope and a new way of safety for their families, and they make a living here and have a normal life, not having to live in fear and extreme poverty." In addition to working with agencies along the border, Buckner officials also are aggressively pursuing other ways to help the government deal with the surge of migrants.

The global village connects us to the reality of the world's poorest most helpless ones as never before. Instant communications puts us at the heart of Christianity today and on display for the whole world to see. The concept of redemption in the Hebrew language comes from the word *goel*, which means kinsman redeemer, the person who stepped in to represent a relative in court, to buy the person back from slavery, to avenge a murder or respond to violence. This person was the nearest relative of another who is charged with the duty of restoring the rights of another and avenging wrongs. For each one of us, God is our Kinsman redeemer. He is our next of kin when we are in trouble. He is our best hope when we have no hope left. In this sense, Buckner does goel-like work for thousands of children and families who have lost their rights and have lost hope. We say, "Hope shines here!"

Redemption in the global village may mean reuniting a baby and his mother. It may mean giving a cup of cold water, a meal, a shower, or a pair of shoes to a family crossing our border without documents. Wherever we have an opportunity to shine hope into the lives of the least of these, we apply our hands and feet in redemptive ways to catch up to what God is doing on the planet.

DISCUSSION QUESTIONS

1. In Deuteronomy 24:17, Moses reminds the people of Israel to care for the widow, the fatherless, and the alien. How does this reminder apply to us today?

2. Why were issues of justice so important to the widow, the fatherless, and the alien during biblical times?

3. How far back do you have to go in your family history to find poverty, economic distress, fatherless children, struggling widows, or immigrants?

4. Name three hot spots in the world today whose conditions have produced widows, vulnerable children, and people migrating to save their own lives. How should we respond?

5. How would you respond to Moses' call to justice, generosity, and redemption?

SEVEN:

Collaborative Redemption, Making the Nations Glad

"May the nations be glad and sing for joy, for you rule the peoples justly and guide the nations of the earth. May all the peoples praise you, O God; may all the peoples praise you."

PSALM 67:4-5

"HOPE SHINES HERE"

There is no doubt in my mind that the question that will define the 21st century is centered on the global conversation rooted in the global question: What is the best way to live life on the planet?[1] I am biased in my perspective on the answer. I adhere to the teachings of Jesus of Nazareth who taught his followers they should "do unto others as they would have them do unto you." This is the Jesus way, the J-shaped worldview[2], the Judeo-Christian worldview. Everywhere I travel across the planet, it is plain to see that the closer things come under the influence of the teachings of Jesus the better they become. Hope tends to spring up in those places. The converse is also true. The farther away things get from the influence of the teachings of Jesus, the worse they tend to become. Everywhere I observe progress and hope emerge, I find that the footprints, the fingerprints, and the fragrance of the presence of Jesus is not far. Robert Cooke Buckner, the founder of Buckner International, was a J-shaped leader. He did J-shaped projects and shined hope into the lives of hurting people. He was at his best when he rallied people of all faiths and no faith to serve the "least of these" in the community and across the state and nation. He was an agent of redemption, a collaborator. My vision for Buckner is to enhance and engage agents of redemption, churches focused on redemptive work in the local and global village, denominational families, Christian agencies, faith-based organizations, Christian universities, Bible colleges, and seminaries, businessmen and women, volunteers and donors to make the nations glad by our collaborative efforts to shine hope across the globe.

The Psalmist says in Psalms 67:4-5, "May the nations be glad and sing for joy, for you rule the peoples justly and guide the nations of the earth. May all the nations praise you, O God, may all the peoples praise you." What could the Psalmist have meant? How would we go about encouraging the nations to be glad? What could cause them to sing for joy? How would God's just rule prevail over the nations of the earth? What would it look like for the nations to be guided by God's hand? What conditions would have to be in place for the nations to praise God? What would have to happen for all the peoples of the earth to praise God? I am not sure about the answers to these questions but some clues may be found in the verses preceding and following Psalm 67:4-5.

The verses preceding this aspiration constitute a prayer requesting God's graciousness; his blessing, and his favor in order that his ways may be known on earth and his salvation be known among all the nations. The pattern of Psalm 67 appears to be a prayer for graciousness, blessing, and favor so that the nations observing God's people will respond in praise of God; in gladness and songs of joy; and the gift of God's justice and guidance of nations and peoples. This prayer is followed by an expectation that the land will yield its harvest; followed by more of God's blessing; and an expectation that all the peoples of the ends of the earth will fear him. The point of this book is that we have a role in participating in God's redemptive work in history. To that extent we have a role as agents of redemption to participate with God in the vision of Psalm 67. It seems reasonable to me that we might be able to see a glimpse of this Kingdom reality on earth, as it is in heaven, if we learned how to work together, to choreograph our actions guided by the Holy Spirit so that the nations might be glad.

To collaborate means to work together. To collaborate with Buckner means to work together for the benefit of a child, a senior, or a family looking for hope by providing assistance and support with a view toward redemptive transformation. While we have a number of ways collaboration takes place, I hope the best ways have yet to be developed. My sense is that much of the work that is done in J-shaped fashion is done in silos and with very little to no coordination and collaboration on a global scale. This becomes a question of stewardship. More often than not, I have observed duplication rather than collaboration resulting in less than excellent stewardship of Kingdom resources. A colleague of mine once said that not all collaboration is good; not all partnerships are meant to be. While I agree with the wisdom of this astute observation, I would like to experiment with collaboration that makes redemptive sense, that increases our stewardship, that extends Kingdom resources, and that benefits those we hope to serve. I believe we can do more together for vulnerable children, orphans, and their families than we can do by ourselves. I also believe that when we choose to collaborate rather than duplicate there is a higher opportunity that the nations may become glad and sing for joy as the graciousness, blessing, and favor that flows to us goes through us to them. In fact, I have seen this kind of gladness and joy in the eyes of children, their families, and in the eyes of global south government leaders at the highest levels. These blessings usually come in the form gifts of time, talent, and treasure.

THE GIFT OF SHOES

A few years ago I led a group of pastors and donors to visit Buckner work in Cairo, Egypt. We had the opportunity to visit the great Pyramids of Giza, to take a cruise down the Nile River, the same river where Moses was laid in a basket as a baby, and we visited a children's home for boys. During our visit to the boys home, we had the opportunity to play soccer with them, to hear their stories, to share a meal, and to serve them by placing shoes on their feet. I led a group of about seven pastors into the chapel with about 20 boys and young men. We explained how we would wash and dry their feet, place a new pair of socks on their feet, followed by a brand new pair of tennis shoes. We had the shoes stacked on the platform at the front of the chapel and the boys eagerly awaited their pair of shoes. We shared a time of singing and testimony and then proceeded to place shoes on their feet. It was a unique experience for the pastors and the boys. We began an orderly process of washing and drying feet but the anticipation of a new pair of shoes turned into lots of excitement and noise. Some of us had to find a new pair of shoes because the pair we picked out did not match the size of the feet. Some boys had their eyes on a certain color or style. We sort of entered into a controlled pandemonium, in a good sense.

The experience was so frenetic and exciting that one of the pastors that I have known for many years stopped me in the middle of the excitement and said to me, "I have served as a pastor for almost 27 years, but I have never been on my knees to wash another person's feet. This is just like what Jesus did. I don't know if I should cry or shout for joy. This is changing my life." I reached over and gave him a hug and said, "We are blessed to serve the least of these, to do what Jesus did." We immediately resumed our activity since the boys were eagerly waiting. This pastor would never be the same. He would never think about ministry and serving others in quite the same way. José Gamez, pastor of Alpha Church in Dallas continues today to lead his church "to serve the least of these" in his community, many of which are of Arab background.

One of the older boys pulled me aside to comment on what the experience meant to him. He said, "The last time anyone ever did this for me was the same day I became a follower of Jesus. The person that told me about Jesus washed my feet to show me the Jesus way as part of my discipleship." This experience brought back the memory of the day he started his journey with Jesus.

For those moments, we saw a glimpse of what it meant to "make the nations glad." This experience was not about Buckner or about Pastor Gamez' church in Dallas. It was about bringing the Kingdom of God very near to these young men and boys through a tangible gift of shoes. It was about being the presence of Jesus to them.

THE GIFT OF LIVESTOCK

On another trip to Ethiopia, I led a group of pastors to visit several cities where Buckner has work including Addis Ababa, Bantu, Debra Zeit, and Axum. On our visit to Bantu, we visited a school built by the generous gifts of Buckner donors. We shared coffee and popcorn made fresh while we visited. We also visited with families served by our Family Hope Center in Bantu. We learned about a family preservation program that provided a $100 grant for families who would normally work the land growing crops and living off the yield of the harvest. These were very poor families. They did not have daily access to milk, cheese, meat, and other foods that most of us expect to eat every day. These items were normally eaten only on special occasions or once a month if they were fortunate.

The group of pastors and I were welcomed by several families with their goats and cows to say thank you to our group. We met fathers, mothers, and children with big smiles on their faces, each patiently waiting in line to greet us and to say "thank you" for changing their lives. They gave profound thanks because they realized that with this grant their families would now have milk, cheese, butter, and meat for generations to come. They said their lives would never be the same. They commented that all the generations of their families before them were poor and limited to eating grain from the field with little expectation of eating commodities such as milk, cheese, butter, and meat, except on rare occasion. With that simple gift their families would experience a whole new level of prosperity, nutrition, and provision. They honored us as though we were kings and princes.

The pastors in our group were stunned with the expression of thanks and even more humbled by hearing the stories of these families who had gathered to say "Amase ganalo," thank you. I will never forget the reaction of one of the pastors from Life Church of San Antonio, a church on the south side of San Antonio, a historically economically challenged area. Obler Robledo, Lead Pastor for the Spanish Congregation at Life Church and associational catalytic missionary for house churches in San Antonio, was with me on that trip. After he realized what the situation was with the families in Bantu, he turned to me and said, "Our church can do something about this. I am going to call the leadership of our small groups right now and challenge them to raise funds for 20 more families." He pulled away from the group and made a phone call to San Antonio from Bantu, Ethiopia and challenged all 20 of the small groups he supervised to raise $100 each to change the future of 20 more families in Bantu. Before we left the country, Obler had 20 commitments to raise $2,000 to help 20 more families with a one-time grant. A few months later, one of our Buckner leaders spoke at Life Church of San Antonio and accepted a check for $2,000 for this program. I don't recall asking Obler to do this. It was a logical, normal, natural, Kingdom sort-of response. I think we made that small part of the nation of Ethiopia glad that day, thanks to Obler's enthusiasm and vision. We helped make the nations glad with the gift of grant to purchase livestock that would change the well-being of that family and future generations.

THE GIFT OF SEEDS

When Emily Candee decided to go on a "Shoes for Orphan Souls" mission trip to Guatemala in 2012, she was ready to conquer the world. With great intentions and high ambitions, she wanted to impact the life of every child she met. During her one-week trip, she was going to change the world.

Fortunately, God used other people and an amazing book called *When Helping Hurts* to teach her about the true meaning of a short-term mission trip before she left. She came to realize that a short-term mission trip is part of a larger plan for the specific community being helped.

There are people who have taken the time to form meaningful relationships enabling them to fully understand the community's specific needs, culture, and worldview. The root causes of a community's issues are understood through that bond, which allows processes to be implemented to stop poverty, heal broken families and address other issues before they begin.

She learned that her job on a short-term mission trip was to continue to plant the seeds to create lasting change in the hearts of the people being served. She knew she might get to see some of the fruit from the seeds she helped sow, but chances were high that it would be years before the "results" were witnessed. Instant gratification, although nice, was not the goal.

At the government-run orphanage in Guatemala, she was fortunate to see the fruit of the seeds someone had sowed before her, and it was her prayer that she continued to plant seeds not only with this particular child, but all the other children God brought into her life during her trip.

While making heart puppets with the 3- to 5-year-old boys during Vacation Bible School, a boy named Victor sat in her lap. Emily gave him a hug and could see the love he felt radiate from his brown eyes. She knew that may be the only hug he received that day, so she held him for a while and let him sit in her lap while he finished his puppet.

Thanks to the many years of grade school and high school Spanish, she was able to ask Victor (in her Texas drawl), "Dónde está Jesús?" Victor stopped coloring his puppet, put down his marker, pointed to the sky and said, "Jesús está en el cielo." Chills covered her body and tears welled up in her eyes as she listened to 3-year-old Victor tell her that Jesus is in heaven. Through his answer, Victor revealed the seeds that had been sown by someone before Emily — someone who may never hear those words from Victor's mouth. That person had sown seeds of Christ and his love in that child.

The true meaning of a short-term mission trip had been revealed to Emily in that moment. It was clear that God's work is not about her, not about her agenda and not about seeking instant gratification; rather, she was to continue to plant seeds and strengthen the foundation that had been started by those before her so that others down the road may witness the work God is doing in Victor and in all of God's other children. Although Emily initially wanted to conquer the world during her short time in Guatemala, she is thankful for moments like the one with Victor, where she got to see the work God was doing in the hearts of those he loves.

Emily gave the gift of time, the gift of a hug, and the gift of shoes. She made the nations glad by spending time with Victor and by watering a seed that had been planted.

THE GIFT OF FAMILY

The simple declaration that a "child has a right to a family" may not sound like a profound statement; it may not seem like a significant affirmation, but it has become reality for thousands of vulnerable children living in Peru. The Peruvian Congress unanimously voted to approve a law in January of 2014 that secures a philosophy of raising a child in a healthy family environment rather than in an institutional setting. Claudia Leon Vergara, Executive Director of Buckner Peru, led the effort to establish a foster care program in her country of origin. Claudia is one of the few Buckner staff in the history of Buckner to affect change at the national level that ultimately benefits vulnerable children.

Claudia has worked for several years to develop the concept of Foster Care for Peru and has implemented a program whereby children can be placed in homes for Foster Care in their own community. Prior to this program, children who experienced abandonment, neglect, or abuse were taken into custody and then sent to a local orphanage. Today, the law in Peru states that prior to being sent to an orphanage, a child may be given the option of being placed with a foster care family. Placing a child in an institutional setting like an orphanage can be damaging to the child's development.

Claudia collaborated with government leaders and leaders of the Peruvian Congress to develop a law that provided for the right of a vulnerable child to a family, assisting the Peruvian Congress to pass a law that integrates foster care into the official legal code of Peru. The new law protects the groundwork laid for foster care in the previous six years through a collaborative relationship between Buckner Peru, Buckner International and INABIF (Peru's National Integral Program for the Well-being of Families). Claudia spearheaded the foster care movement in 2007 when she initiated an agreement between Buckner and the Peruvian government. The first children were placed in foster homes in 2008. Since then, a total of 44 children have been placed in foster care.

The foster care legal code approved on December 5, 2013 will provide stability and assurance that foster care will be available to vulnerable children regardless of the change of the political party elected to office. The new law is the best way to ensure children's rights are protected, and it raises the potential for children to be placed into foster homes rather than in institutional care. Before the introduction of foster care, institutions were the only care option for vulnerable and orphan children in Peru. Early childhood experts say that for every three months a young child lives in an institution, they lose a month of physical, mental and psychosocial development. The average orphanage stay in Peru is five years, and many children live in institutional settings until they age out at 18 years of age. Impacting the laws and policies and procedures also impacts the quality of care and the outcome for these children and families to be more successful. It took one person, one leader, Claudia Leon, to have a vision for the future of her country to make "the nations glad." Foster care was a foreign concept in Latin America when Claudia began promoting it as a solution for Peru's vulnerable children. Conventional wisdom concluded foster care wouldn't be culturally accepted, but over the years attitudes throughout Latin America have gradually began to shift.

While in Peru during a Buckner International board trip, I met with Ms. Nancy Tolentino, Director of INABIF, National Institution for the Welfare of Infants, to present two of three books written by Claudia and her staff. The first book introduced the concept and procedure of Foster Care. Books two and three were training manuals for social workers and professionals working with children, and a manual for training parents involved in social work. We were greeted by Marisol Espinoza, Vice President of Peru, who delivered remarks to the Buckner board members and leaders, agency heads, professionals, and government leaders. She commended Buckner Peru for its collaborative efforts with the Peruvian government.

Buckner has introduced and helped to develop foster care in Russia (along with Children's Hope Chest), Peru, Honduras, and Kenya. Claudia continues to plant the seeds of family throughout Latin America. She was invited to provide foster care training in Argentina in 2008, Honduras and Guatemala in 2010, Guyana in 2012, and the Dominican Republic, Ecuador and Mexico in 2013. The Dominican Republic government is currently working on technical instruments and policy guidelines to make foster care a government option by 2014. This is the legacy of our founder who among other things, wrote the child labor laws in Texas and helped to shape the federal child labor laws in the United States. Our staff serves individual children and families but we also work to lead change in social systems through collaborative efforts with national leaders of other countries. Collaboration between our staff and international leaders has resulted in making "nations glad" with the gift of family. It is the vision of the greater good, of bringing the Kingdom near, that tends to make nations glad.

THE GIFT OF MINISTRY COLLABORATION

One of the most challenging yet rewarding forms of Kingdom collaboration is when independent Christian or faith-based agencies collaborate for superior stewardship and transformation. When it makes sense to collaborate in complementary fashion, two agencies working together in the same community or city can make exponential impact by creating a seamless and comprehensive set of solutions for children and families in need. For several years we have enjoyed a collaborative relationship with International Justice Mission in Guatemala. We complement each other's work and provide a comprehensive solution for girls engaged in human trafficking and sexual exploitation. At the writing of this book, I am in conversation with a Christian agency that works in the same country as Buckner does to discover how we might collaborate to benefit vulnerable children and their families. I am in conversation with a Christian university to explore ways we might engage students in global mission with Buckner to make a transformational impact and engage their students in projects that enhance their educational experience. I am also in conversation with a denominational family to explore ways we might engage congregations in global mission with Buckner. I realize any collaboration that will be blessed by God must be led by the Holy Spirit and done in humility. The gift of ministry collaboration not only results in superior stewardship but also demonstrates uncommon unity that stands apart as a marker of the J-shaped way.

DISCUSSION QUESTIONS

1. In Psalm 67:4-5, the Psalmist David suggests that the nations become glad because the Lord rules justly. What part do we have in living out justice in the lives of the least of these around us?

2. How does the Lord guide the nations of the earth?

3. When nations experience justice and guidance from the Lord, how does that lead to gladness?

4. What are some ways your church, small group, or church network might collaborate to make a difference in the world among vulnerable children and orphans?

5. Which of the following gifts do you resonate with the most: Shoes, Goats, Spiritual Seeds, or the gift of Family? Why?

EIGHT:

Profile in Compassion: Dickson Masindano

"See, I have engraved you on the palms of my hands; your walls are ever before me."

ISAIAH 49:16 NIV

My first extended time getting to know Dickson Masindano was in Kenya during a magnificently orchestrated 10th anniversary celebration in the summer of 2011 for Buckner Kenya at the Baptist Childrens Center (BCC) in Nairobi. He planned for a Master of Ceremonies, lots of African music, full of praise and worship. During that week we visited Buckner-Kenya work in Nairobi, Busia, Kitale, and Bungoma. At the end of the week, children from those cities gathered with us to celebrate the 10th anniversary in their native dress to present music, dance, poems, and scripture. Her Excellency, Madam Pauline Kalonzo, 2nd Lady of Kenya (wife of the Vice President) was on hand to share in the celebration and share some comments. She commended the work of Buckner in Kenya, the Buckner Kenya Staff, and the Kenya Baptist Convention for their excellent work, perseverance, and vision. She called for spreading Buckner work across other cities in Kenya and challenged the crowd to replicate the work of Buckner so other children and families would be blessed by this redemptive ministry.

Pastor David Keatu, member of the BCC Board of Directors told the story of how the work was begun. He told how the pastors and officers of the Kenya Baptist Convention (in the late 1990s) representing about 3,000 Kenyan Baptist churches, decided to secure and convey 13.5 acres of land for use to serve vulnerable children and orphans as a Kingdom ministry. After much deliberation, the officers of the Kenyan Baptist Convention (KBC) agreed to this action. Pastor Keatu was among the leaders during this time of decision. The land was given to the KBC by the Kenyan Government as long as it would be used to serve under-served children and orphans. This is a fascinating story of the pastors, churches, and the convention of churches deciding to put the needs of the least of these before their interests.

The Southern Baptist Convention's International Mission Board operated the BCC from 1994 until 2002 when Buckner assumed responsibility for the operations under the leadership of Dr. Ken Hall then CEO of Buckner. Later, Canadian Baptists, the Cooperative Baptist Fellowship as well as countless Texas Baptist churches and other like-minded churches and volunteers came together to add to the story. The story of the BCC is a story of pastors, individuals, volunteers, churches, and denominational groups working together in an unselfish way to advance redemptive work in the lives of vulnerable children and their families in this great nation.

I left the 10th anniversary with a clear impression that the accomplishments of the previous 10 years was driven by a strong, visionary leader with compassion and calling, an agent of redemption. I saw first-hand, the fruits of the work of Dickson Masindano. Dickson is an agent of redemption with a heart full of compassion for the poorest of the poor, the least of these among us in the great nation of Kenya. This is his story of compassion.

Dickson, known as Nate by his village friends, grew up in the northern rift of Kenya. Nate is short-hand for Natembeya, his given middle name, means "walking." He was given this name because he was born while his mother was taking an evening walk to the river to draw water. Dickson was orphaned at the age of eight because his mother, Miriam Namachanja, contracted an incurable case of malaria. In honor of the memory of his mother, Dickson named his first born daughter after his mother, Miriam. He grew up with one brother and nine step-siblings from his father's marriage and lived with his maternal grandparents in a village near Mount Elgon until he was 15 years of age when he was re-united with this father. His grandfather was a devout Catholic Christian with a basic primary education and practiced polygamy with three wives.

Dickson's father often told Dickson that he was his second grandchild, and that he wanted Dickson to have the best education possible. On his death-bed in 1990, Dickson's father encouraged him to keep going to school because one day God would use his education to improve the village.

JOURNEY TOWARD REDEMPTION

As a young boy, Dickson served as an altar boy in the local Catholic Church in his village. He also spent lots of time learning and playing basketball in school while he lived with his grandparents. He began a friendship with his basketball coach. As they began to get acquainted, Dickson learned that his basketball coach was the son of a Baptist missionary family in the town of Kitale. During a school vacation, Dickson's coach invited him to his home. During that visit the coach's father began talking to Dickson about Jesus Christ and the salvation he provides. During subsequent school holidays, Dickson visited the Baptist church in Kitale and often would visit the Salvation Army church in another village. One day after a session of basketball, the Baptist missionary involved the boys in a Bible competition and awarded the winners with a basketball. The goal of the contest was to recite Bible verses. The best recital of verses would generate better chances of winning. Over time, Dickson began to enjoy the Bible competition so much that he ended up with "half the Bible in my head." It was only a matter of time that he dropped to his knees to pray to receive Jesus Christ as his savior.

Dickson later joined the Christian union in high school and in college. He was a frequent visitor of the Parklands Baptist church, a charismatic congregation. It was in that church that Dickson began to understand more about God and reflect more on his life. He remembers being a teen, full of strength with a strong desire to dance and jump when given the opportunity. Upon reflection of his life, Dickson became a witness to many promises he had heard preached or read in the Bible that were fulfilled in his life. He summarized his life by saying "at the end of the day, the only thing that matters is doing what God leads you to do."

Dickson will take all the help he can get for the Buckner International ministries he oversees in Kenya. But he wants you to know his goal is less, not more. Ask Dickson where he's headed with Buckner Kenya, which opened ministries here in 2001, and the passion pours out of him. "It's all about self-sustainability," he says. "Our goal is to do more with less." And by less, he's talking about less dependency on outside sources of revenue to keep operations going. That's why the Buckner ministries in Kenya are diversifying and developing strategies that can stand on their own. From the urban city of Nairobi to rural communities like Kitale, Busia, and Bungoma, the Buckner Kenya staff is planting crops, generating bio-fuel by recycling cow dung, and operating health clinics that charge nominal, but cost-recovery fees for their services.

As the Buckner ministries in Kenya have grown over the past decade, the need to find additional sources of income has also grown. Today, the Buckner Kenya staff includes more than 80 employees, from house parents at the two orphanages, to farm workers and school teachers. It includes nurses, social workers, counselors, cooks, and accountants. Buckner Kenya started like Buckner's work in so many other places — at the request of an existing organization. The Baptist Children's Center in Nairobi opened in 1989, the result of several groups coming together as the wave of orphans from AIDS/HIV was starting to hit Africa.

By the late 1990s, leaders at BCC realized they needed professional advice on running the orphanage. That's when they heard about Buckner and asked for help. When Buckner International staff from Dallas visited BCC in 2000, it was home to about 60 children living in two crammed houses. And while the BCC staff did the best they could, it was obvious the children's home needed help. That's when Dickson showed up from Abilene, Texas. He was finishing his master's degree at Hardin-Simmons University and was headed back to his home country when he was introduced to Buckner. By the time he got on an airplane bound for Kenya, Dickson was the first Buckner Kenya employee. The NGO (non-governmental organization) application was filed in 2000 and in 2001, Buckner Kenya became operational with the BCC as its first ministry.

Today, the campus of BCC is a bustling hive of activity. While the orphanage is the mainstay of the work, the site is also home to Munyao Memorial Baptist Chapel, Baptist Health Clinic, a school for 300 children from the nearby Mali Saba slum, a technology education center, and a farm. Along with the work taking place at the BCC campus,

Buckner also sponsors about 90 children in foster and kinship care throughout Nairobi. Add that to the 22 children living at the orphanage and Buckner has more than 110 children in residential care on any given day in the city, far more than 10 years ago, but with far fewer living in an institutional setting, always a goal of Buckner ministries.

The children living at the orphanage today are among the most vulnerable children in Nairobi. Many of them have been abused or neglected. Many are orphans due to the death of their parents from AIDS. The goal of the BCC is to keep the children at BCC for as little as possible and then place them in families. Like the Buckner programs themselves, Dickson wants the children and families served to become self-sustaining as soon as possible. To accomplish that goal, the orphanage has become more of an assessment center where the children are cared for and counseled while the Buckner staff determines the best place for each child. Most of the children move from BCC to foster or kinship care, where they live with a trained foster family or with relatives, all under continued monitoring from Buckner caseworkers.

Dickson believes a child should be able to look back and say, "If it were not for Buckner, where would I be?" Dickson wants to give them an inheritance, because in Africa, an inheritance is very important and he believes we can give them an inheritance of a basic education. That inheritance is also being offered for children living near BCC who attend the center's school. The families pay a school fee — what Dickson calls "cost sharing." The school enables Buckner to reach into the entire community. And while Dickson emphasizes self-sustaining models for Buckner and the families they serve, they want groups from the United States to know they are still desperately needed in Kenya. Dickson encourages groups to keep coming and providing medical, technical and educational support. He says, "That's very, very important. Sometimes the most important thing you can do is just play with the children and spend time with them. It's not how much we give, but how much love is in the giving. We need people to keep coming and giving that love." Dickson's compassion is deep in Nairobi but also spreads across the country of Kenya to Kitale.

PLANTING SEEDS OF HOPE

Dickson has also made a big difference in Kitale, Kenya. Sammy Nyongesa estimates the tomatoes growing in the greenhouse at Seed of Hope Orphanage in Kitale will top 2,600 lbs. a year. More than 40 acres of maize and beans encircle the children's home and in a stall at the back of the campus are two new calves that will soon join the growing herd of cows that furnish milk for many children.

Sammy is the farm manager at Seed of Hope and the work he and his crew do is moving the orphanage and its ministries closer to self-sustainability. Director Esther Ngure is creating independence for the Seed of Hope ministries in Kitale and the children who live there. Located in the northern part of Kenya, Seed of Hope was founded by German evangelical missionary Carsten Warner. Three years ago, Carsten approached Buckner about taking over the ministries when he moved back to Germany, with the promise that he would continue raising support for the work — a promise he is keeping.

Since then, Buckner has expanded the work in and around Kitale. Current ministries include the Seed of Hope orphanage; foster and kinship care; two medical clinics; a school for children in grades 1-8; an early childhood center known as the Kay School after Roy Kay, grandfather of donor Katy Reynolds; a church located on the school grounds; and the 40-acre farm.

Christopher is a 16-year-old who has lived at Seed of Hope for seven years and says,. "In 2002, when I came, I lived with my grandmom, and I was not going to school. I did not even know what a school was. But the way I am living with Seed of Hope is the way I was living with my parents. I took them as my mother and father. They have become my protectors and they are teaching me the Word of God. Moses Simiyu and Robert Namsale and Esther (Ngure), our manager, those are my favorite parents because they are born again Christians and they are advising me to succeed."

It is patterned after similar Buckner ministries in Nairobi and Busia, where health nurse Gladys Barasa says the greatest "need of the population is getting education. Most of the people from the interior still think that malaria comes from the rain. It is a parasitic infection." As she speaks, Catherine, a small girl in the next room is being treated for malaria. "Most of the cases are in children," she said. "It's very common in children here. We're here to enlighten the community and tell them about them. Barasa said that through support the Buckner Community Development Center receives from churches such as Wilshire Baptist Church in Dallas, the center has attracted residents from as far as 20 miles away. "But we need to expand the medical clinic here," she added. "For the children who come here, my wish is…this is a semi-arid place…if we had more food…most of the children are malnourished. If we had more food it would be a good thing."

Nearby in the village of Cherangani, Buckner opened the Herbert H. Reynolds Ministry Center, which serves as a pre-school for neighboring children, houses the foster/kinship care staff that oversees more than 50 children in the community, a water well for the community, and the Greater Zion Medical Center, built by the Greater Mount Baptist Church in Forth Worth. Esther said about 70 children live at the Seed of Hope Orphanage. They are children "whose extended families are unable to care for them," she said. And while the campus is the center of ministry for Buckner's work in Kitale, multiple programs serving the community extend the ministry's reach far beyond the orphanage. Programs like "Home Based Care" enable needy families to receive support. Currently 12 families, mostly parents who are HIV positive, are receiving assistance, expanding Buckner's care for children to 20 more.

Esther says, "The goal is to ease the burden of the families who have a heart to help their children, but don't have the financial support to take care of the children." That small investment allows the children to stay with their families rather than being moved to an orphanage or left homeless. She added that the hope is to have "well-balanced children who become good parents who are able to stand on their own as adults." The compassion found in Esther Ngure is a contagious spirit that comes from Dickson and extends to students like Ben and Rachel.

DRIVEN BY COMPASSION

Ben, 20, sits on the edge of his bed at the Buckner Transitional Home in Nairobi. He is a citizen of two worlds, and his room shows it. Pictures of Western entertainers cut out from magazines surround his bed, while a Bible sits on his nightstand. He speaks quietly of the heartaches and joys of his past and the promise of his future. His story is one of change and hope, a story that Buckner has been a part of for years. "In the beginning I was a street boy, when my mother died in 1992," he said. I went to (another children's home), then the Baptist Children's Center at the age of 6. Life is so difficult on the street because there is no food, no shelter, and no clothes. The Baptist Children's Center offered food, clothes, shelter." But those three staples were not enough for a young child used to running free, he said. "At first, I used to escape and go back to the street. It was so difficult for me to stay at the Baptist Children's Center because I was not used to staying in one place. But a pastor gave us counseling and told us about Jesus Christ and said, 'Do not go back to the street.'"

Ben accepted Christ at that point and gave up some of the street practices he'd learned early. "I stopped sniffing glue and escaping from

BCC and my education improved. In our day, there were so, so many street boys at Baptist Children's Center." The Baptist Children's Center, supported in part by Buckner, lies in an impoverished area in Nairobi. In addition to an orphanage, it provides a community center, school and medical clinic. For many children, it also has been a life-preserving oasis. "Life there was so fun," he said. "We went to school Monday through Friday and Saturday was visiting day. People would bring us some good things. We played games. My favorite dorm parent was Joseph. When I was small, he used to wash my clothes, and give me food."

When asked what life would be like without the center, he grows reflective. "Without it, I don't think I would be alive, I would end up being killed. My brother Richard remained a street kid. He was killed last year in April when I was in the 12th grade. He went to steal in a bank and was killed. He was 22." While he remembers the past, his eyes look to his future, one being ushered in by the transitional home. "Here we cook for ourselves. Here we can do our own thing. Here, you have to choose for yourself."

The three boys currently at the transitional home are engaged in church and school, Ben says. "Church is so good. There is an active youth ministry. I want to do auto management and get a good job. I live here because one day God is going to provide for me. I'm going to have my own family. My future is so, so good because one thing I know: I have a vision. When I get money, I want to start my own children's home." That sharing spirit, he said, comes from years of support from Buckner. "I learned to share. The donors from the U.S.A. used to share and bring something of their own. Some of them would come in August and December, so they would bring us good things and leave good things with (Buckner country director) Dickson (Masindano) to share. When we were together it used to feel like we were one family." One volunteer in particular, changed his life, he said. "There was one called Bob (Hefner, of Dallas). When he would come, he would usually tell us about being good, about Jesus Christ. We were so happy when he would come. He would tell us about reality, what is going to happen."

Rachel, a pre-teen girl, enrolled at the BCC school escaped the violence that struck Kenya in early 2008 following political elections in the country. "I am from the (another) province. Because of the political violence, I came here in February. I praise the Lord for the place here. I know that when I come out of this place. I will be able to live a life again. "I don't have my parents here. They are far," she said. "I am not comfortable with life because of the post-election violence, but I bless the Lord because our manager here treats us well. If would not be here, it would be bad because of life outside.

"Outside, with nothing to do, is the devil's workshop," Rachel said. "Every day we are welcome here. They teach us the word of God."

10 YEARS AND COUNTING

Ten years after he started all this in Kenya for Buckner, Dickson knows the key for the next 10 years and beyond is self-sustainability, wherever Buckner starts new programs. That remains a primary criterion for him. "We need to do that for the betterment of ourselves," he said. "If you're not doing something about self-sustainability, you will just leave empty buildings." And even with the growth of Buckner programs over the past 10 years, Dickson remains intent on doing more. "What we've done is just a drop in the ocean," he said. "We've simply got to continue playing our part in the lives of vulnerable children. As much as we're doing things right, we can still do better."

At the core of Dickson's heart is the determination that children in Kenya and everywhere deserve the basic rights of education, food, health care, and protection. "Kids are so exposed to the dangers of the world," he said. "A child should be able to look back and say, 'If it were not for Buckner, where would I be?'

"We're at our best when we do what we do best," he added, "just helping each child one at a time." Dickson is an agent of redemption driven by a spirit of compassion for the children he serves in Kenya.

DISCUSSION QUESTIONS

1. In Isaiah 49:16, the Prophet Isaiah says that God has grafted us into the palms of his own hands and a wall of protection is a constant reminder. How does this verse and truth intersect with Dickson's life and with those he serves?

2. How does this verse connect to the truth that Paul spoke of in Romans 8:28-39?

3. Where does the compassion that drives Dickson come from?

4. What would the Lord lead you, your group, your church, your church network to do in response to the needs of the vulnerable children and orphans in Kenya?

5. After reading Dickson's story, what do you feel led to pray about today?

NINE:

Profile in Conviction: Cynthia Blake Rentie

"I can do everything through him who gives me strength."

PHILIPPIANS 4:13 NIV

I could not stop the flow of tears that began to flow down my face the day I heard a Buckner client say, "Buckner was the first place in my life where I ever heard of the concept of grace." I listened to the young and courageous mom talk about her life, her past, and her recovery through the Family Pathways program in Dallas, Texas. If all we were able to do was to give her and her children a safe family environment and a bright future, it would be enough to have a grand celebration and come to the conclusion that our efforts are not in vain. Truly this work is a high and worthy goal. However, the story does not stop there. Beyond the provision of a new start, acceptance, and recovery are the multiple stories of redemption of whole lives that continue to emerge from the Family Pathways program in Dallas and throughout Texas.

I have come to realize that behind every great program is an outstanding visionary leader who is called to do this work, gifted in the ministry of restoration, and deeply faith-integrated in approach. She has the perfect blend of leadership, management, social service, and ministry skills. She has the faith heritage and vision of our founder deep in her heart. She is a deeply spiritual and faith-filled person with an uncommon passion and conviction to serve hurting moms, to believe in them, to gently challenge them and insist on their best.

I first met Cynthia about 2009 during a conversation in my office. She was interviewing me as part of our talent management program. I was impressed with her the very first time we met. She was gregarious, energetic, enthusiastic, and passionate about her work. She struck me as a person full of conviction. You cannot be around Cynthia any amount of time without hearing about her convictions and faith orientation. This is her story.

Cynthia Blake Rentie was born in Rockford, Illinois, the fourth child of six children born to James and Dorothy Blake. Her father was a construction worker and her mother worked for a linen factory in Rockford, and also attended cosmetology school because her dream was to have her own hair salon. The winters in Rockford and the financial stress on the family made it difficult for her father to provide for the family. Her father was a wonderful Christian man of great faith, who took great value in providing for his family. On one particularly harsh winter day, Cynthia's dad said to her mom, "Jean (her middle name), we have $500 to our name and can stay and fight through this winter, or we can leave and move to Oklahoma, live with my parents and find work so that I can take care of my family." Her mom told her dad that her place is with him, as a family. Cynthia remembers the family being in a circle, holding hands, on the final day in their Rockford home, with her daddy praying. Her dad was a faithful praying man; believing that "A family that prays together, stays together."

So the next day they packed up the car with what could fit and they left for Oklahoma in 1969, with their four-year old daughter, Cynthia, and the rest of the family. It is amazing how much she remembers about Rockford being so young. Cynthia remembers looking through the back window as the family drove away from their home; with a sad heart because for some reason she knew she would never see her best friend, Cynthia Brown, anymore. She held on tight to her doll, named Mrs. Beasly, with sadness in her heart. There was so much snow on the ground that day but she wasn't worried because her daddy was like Superman to her; he could get through anything. Two days later they arrived in Oklahoma and a new journey began.

JOURNEY TOWARD REDEMPTION

Cynthia's journey toward redemption started with wonderful parents who taught her and her five siblings the importance of honoring God's word by being children of integrity, honesty, love, and passion to service. She grew up monetarily poor, but unaware of her low social economic status, because she was so rich with love. The one thing that Cynthia loves most about her parents is that even though their funds were limited, they never wavered when it came to paying their tithes. They had such a strong spiritual foundation of faith and commitment to be agents for the Lord. They received so much joy out of serving in the church and in the community. Her dad served as a deacon in the church and her mother played the piano for the church and served as deaconess. They believed and taught their children to love God first, each other and always be ready to help those in need. Her dad would tell the children to remember where they came from because it sets the path for where they are going.

When her dad died in a car accident in 2002, the family could not have survived were it not for their faith and understanding that God is in control. When she arrived in Oklahoma after receiving the news about the accident, she looked at his truck in the yard, bawling her eyes out, trying to piece together that her father was gone. For the first time she asked God why? How could he take such a great man from them, when there were a lot of bad people he could have chosen instead? Then Proverbs 3:5 came to her as she was crying: "Trust in the Lord with all your heart, lean not on your own understanding." She knew as she stood there that her father was sending her the answer from heaven to give her comfort and reminding her God is in control. Her love for the Lord is so great, and her faith in his word is strong because of the foundation she grew up on; raised by parents of great faith and love for God, each other and family. Her siblings share those same Christian values that were rooted in them by their parents since they were little. She has three wonderful brothers today who are gifted in sharing the gospel in any capacity; whether at work, church, or home. She also has two sweet sisters, who bring joy and happiness to all those they encounter.

LEADING WITH CONVICTION AND TRANSFORMING LIVES

Cynthia's career as a basketball athlete at Cameron University in Lawton, Oklahoma informs her service at Buckner. She knows what it is like to lead a team, to encourage other players, and to work toward a goal, a victory. This spirit of victory comes from a deeply held set of convictions. She leads with conviction and encourages mothers facing very difficult days. Dark days filled with discouragement, betrayal, and disappointment. Cynthia works toward the transformation of moms like Kimberly Evans, Robin Cole, Karin Espiricueta, and Leslie Melton.

The road a single mom travels can sometimes be overwhelming and dark. The clients at Family Pathways tend to be single moms struggling to provide, and their roads filled with potholes — unpaid bills, little mouths to feed and employers that require higher education which, due to responsibilities, they could not attain. But Buckner Family Pathways, a self-sufficiency program based in Dallas, is out on the road in front of the group, filling in potholes with things like rental subsidies and childcare, making the road-of-life a little smoother.

On a hot day in June, five graduates from the Family Pathways program were honored at a graduation brunch for their accomplishments. Each woman stood up, with tears in their eyes and gave a testimony of their life-changing experience. "I have never been one to finish anything," Kimberly Evans said. "But today I stand before you and I have finished. I never knew what God had for me, but now I know — I am meant to be a teacher." Women who thought they would never get the opportunity to work for an academic diploma have gone above and beyond. "I've already got my degree and I'm going for another one," Robin Cole said. "I'm very thankful that Family Pathways helped me meet my challenge."

Karina Espiricueta, a recent graduate, used to live with her two children and her mother. She never believed that she could make a better life for herself. "The best thing about Buckner Family Pathways is the encouragement from the staff," she said. "Every time they see us, the encourage us, saying things like, 'You can do it.'" In the past she had daunting jobs with odd hours and thought she could never get anything better, she said. But now, "I have the confidence that I can do whatever I want." Espiricueta is now moving from Family Pathways into her own apartment and will begin saving money to make a down payment on a house for her family. She earned her degree as a Licensed Vocational Nurse, something she never could have done without the support of Buckner, she said.

Leslie Melton, another graduate, also mentioned the life-changing role Buckner played in her 4-year-old daughter Emily's life. "Family

Pathways gave my daughter the opportunity to have a normal life," Melton said. Before entering the program, Melton and her baby lived in a halfway house in Oak Cliff. She was trying to recover from a long battle with drug abuse and had nowhere else to go. About 17 female drug users lived in the three-bedroom house at any given time — a dangerous environment for her and her baby, she said. "This place is all about the kids," Melton said, after explaining about all the activities, opportunities and attention the children receive. This past year, her daughter Emily was surprised with Christmas presents, a new and exciting experience for her, she said.

As Melton shared details and stories about her hardships in the past, she admitted that she had some trust issues. When she first heard about the program, it was hard for her to believe that anyone would want to help her without expecting something in return. "Everyone was so nice. I wondered what they were up to," she said with a laugh. "But after being at Family Pathways I've learned that not everyone is out to get you." Melton admitted that she has spent many years "on the opposite side of the law," but now, after earning her degree in criminal justice, she plans to become a probation officer to help people like her former self. "I'm so proud of me," she said. "Anyone that knows me, where I've been and where I've come from, would be proud of me, too."

The road for these graduates used to be a roundabout, but Buckner provided an exit ramp. And now, after their hard work and perseverance, they are on a road that is headed straight for their dreams. "This program will definitely help those who want to do something with their lives because the support is extraordinary," Espiricueta said.

LEADING FAMILY PATHWAYS IN DALLAS, TEXAS

The best thing Cynthia likes about leading Family Pathways is the healing, restoration, and hope provided to many individuals using Christian principles ministered with professional competence, grace, and compassion. She loves that fact she gets to see the work of the Lord happening each day as clients experience change and hope. She loves working in a place that gives an opportunity for the lost or broken to be redeemed and for transformation of lives through the services Buckner offers. She loves the experience of observing true discipleship through engagement with donors, volunteers, and staff; and a true desire is to be change agents for God. The moms in the program often state how it makes them happy to know there are people who care without expecting anything in return; how Buckner is a place of refuge from their hurts, habits, and hang ups; a place where they can heal and experience the mercy and grace from God for themselves.

Family Pathways is a place where clients are not judged, but instead are supported spiritually. She loves that Family Pathways is a place where prayer is welcomed and often used as a powerful healing tool for clients and staff; the word of God is a driving force for bringing about change and growth. The opportunity of serving as an agent of redemption, planting the seeds of the gospel into the wounded spirits of clients and watching them grow is a huge blessing. Helping clients pull away the weeds that kept them from blossoming into beautiful flowers of redemption, by constantly reminding them that God loves them, no matter what happened in their past, talking about God's love, forgiveness, and forgiving themselves is one of the great blessings of this ministry. Cynthia leads this ministry by example. She is an example of an overcomer; an example of a leader that leads by conviction, by faith.

DISCUSSION QUESTIONS

1. In Philippians 4:13, the Apostle Paul says he can do all things through Christ who strengthens him. How is this truth evident in the ministry of Cynthia Rentie?

2. What were some of the key factors that formed Cynthia's faith and conviction?

3. Cynthia is driven by a conviction that with God, all things are possible. How critical is that kind of faith when serving as an agent of redemption?

4. What would the Lord lead you, your group, your church; your church network to do in response to the needs of abused mothers and their children?

5. After reading Cynthia's story, how do you feel led to pray today?

TEN:

Profile in Courage: Claudia Leon Vergara

"Have I not commanded you? Be strong and courageous. Do not be afraid; do not be discouraged, for the Lord your God will be with you wherever you go."

JOSHUA 1:9

I have come to believe everything, including progress and success in ministry, rises or falls on leadership. Courageous leaders are full of a personal sense of mission, passion, and vision for what might be in the future. Buckner is blessed in many ways. One of the ways we are magnificently blessed is with the quality of leadership the Lord has brought to us. We seem to attract leaders with deep compassion, conviction, and courage. One of the outstanding leaders we are blessed with is Claudia Leon Vergara. I met Claudia in 2008 after she became Executive Director of Buckner-Peru. We met in Dallas during one of her visits to an annual leadership conference during Founder's Week in April of that year.

While meeting Claudia in 2008 was encouraging and learning of her excellent work was very exciting, nothing could have impressed me more than my first visit to Peru in 2013. I led a group of pastors and leaders to tour Buckner work in Peru during a week long trip to Lima and Cuzco. The group of pastors and leaders immediately affirmed Claudia's leadership, the quality of her team, and the excellence in the programs she led. Claudia is an exemplary leader, an outstanding professional and exceptional change agent. Since the day I met her, I kept telling her that I was planning to visit Peru to review her work. She patiently waited, smiled politely, and kept my promise in mind. When I finally arrived, her team greeted our delegation with great enthusiasm and warmth. We were greeted in royal fashion, toured the Presidential Palace, had lunch with Marisol Espinoza, the Vice President of the country, toured Buckner work in Lima and Cuzco, Occoran, and made our way to Machu Picchu. I quickly came to appreciate Claudia as a courageous change agent and leader, par excellence. This is her story of redemption and courage.

Claudia Leon Vergara was born on March 4, 1975 in the city of Lima, Peru. She is the daughter of two very special people who have definitely had a big influence in her life. Her father, Rafael Leon, was a doctor of nephrology and a native of Piura, a city in northern Peru. Her mother, Elena Vergara, was a teacher by profession and then later devoted herself to business. Claudia has a sister named Karina that is two and a half years older. Her father served in the Peruvian Army as a doctor and was diagnosed with lymphatic cancer at the young age of 30. His healing provided another 16 years of life. One of her father's dreams was to open a dialysis center in Piura, his native city. Claudia remembers as a five year old, moving to Piura with her family to fulfill her father's life-long dream. She remembers serving the community with her father, delivering turkeys and gifts to humble people that received free treatments from her father. When criticized for not collecting fees from patients, Dr. Leon would explain that a life was priceless and if he did not treat people with no money, they would not live. Claudia remembers this as one of her best memories of generosity and the value that every human being carries. This spirit of dignity and value for every human being drives Claudia in her mission at Buckner. Her courageous leadership and influence has helped to transform the lives of many people. The following are glimpses of how Claudia has impacted the lives of Yanet Casares, Mary Cruz Romera, Melba Moran, and Ursula Elena Perez Ascona.

LEADING WITH COURAGE TO TRANSFORM LIVES
YANET CACERES

Yanet Caceres rose every morning, put on worn-down shoes and left her still-sleeping family. She emerged from her house, a shack with dirt floors, cinderblock walls and a tin roof, with an empty five-gallon bucket. Climbing down 50 yards of steep, rickety stairs built in the dusty hillside, she made her way down to the main path. She walked to the public water barrel, filled her bucket and headed back up the stairs. Back home, she would empty the bucket into a plastic barrel in the corner of her tiny, dirty kitchen. With several neighbors raising pigs in the back of their homes, sanitation was never an option. Day in and day out, she repeated her morning ritual. She climbed back up the stairs with the loaded bucket. She went back down. And back up. And down. And up. And down. And up.

She spent half a day collecting unsafe water for her family. By time she got home, her four kids were up and running around, and she was exhausted. The water they would use the rest of the day for cooking and drinking was dirty and often contained human and dog waste. "We were always sick," she said, her body heavy with the memory. Yanet's home is in Talleres Artesanales, one of the poorest communities in

Lima, where most families make their living raising pigs. Packs of wild dogs roam the sandy hills, packed with houses of cinderblock, tin and bed sheets as doors. The community has a sense of hopelessness hanging over it, but for Yanet and her family, there is one tiny ray they cling to: the water filter they earned from the Buckner Family Hope Center in Pamplona.

Claudia led the effort to provide water filters when she realized the families were using dirty water. The only way to use clean water was for them to make the trip down the hill to purchase clean water. The distance and the cost made it practically impossible for these families to use clean water to drink and to cook with. A blood analysis of the children living in Pamplona showed four different types of parasites in their blood. Claudia knew she had to do something about this. She contacted Matt Asato, Sr. Director of Volunteer Engagement for Buckner, to secure water filters. Once secured, Claudia held a training session with families that included how to use the filters, how to keep them clean, and how to create a sanitary environment. The water filters have made a tremendous improvement in the quality of life for these families.

And now they're not as sick as they used to be. Yanet no longer spends half of her day collecting water. Now she can cook, spend time with her family and help in her community. The Hope Center sits on a hilltop at the edge of Pamplona, right next to the wall that divides the wealthier part of the city from the poor. The bright blue Buckner Peru building sticks out among all the brown and gray that surrounds it, beckoning families to enter.

Buckner Peru has started an initiative based on prevention — strengthening families to keep them together so children don't end up in orphanages. As of the summer of 2014, they're working with 85 families. Claudia recognizes that most of the families are in extreme poverty, and there is a lack of education. Also, most families are repeating the cycles they grew up in. They grew up in violent environments and now are repeating the same thing. Claudia and her team are working to break those cycles and give the families the tools to face life in a different way. They also work with the children so they don't have to go down that same path. Claudia estimates that when Buckner first started work in the community, about 90 percent of homes experienced domestic violence. She said many people didn't know insulting and punching their children were forms of violence because that's how the parents were raised. Buckner staff, under Claudia's leadership, wants to give families the tools to change their lives and they're doing so in a small space with limited resources. But her goal is to develop healthy families.

One priority of the healthy family program is spiritual enrichment. One of Claudia's team members, Giugliana (Julie) Mendoza, the spiritual enrichment and missions coordinator, contends the number one spiritual need in the community is "knowing who they are and what God says about who they are. It's not based on what you do or how much you make because that can change. Who you are in God does not." Claudia notices a lot of spiritual needs. She says, "It's very sad when you meet people who are lacking hope. It's very important for us to work with them and give them a spiritual education to help them develop a personal relationship with Jesus."

Another priority is to help children excel in school so the staff created an after-school program. When the program first started, Claudia says kids in fourth grade read about 20 words a minute and weren't doing well in school. Now, their grades are better and a lot of them actually like going to school.

Claudia's staff is also working with parents to develop skills they can use to make money for their families. They're teaching women to have higher self-esteem and not to allow violence to happen in their homes. Claudia has noticed that domestic violence has decreased in recent years. When reflecting on her work in Peru, Claudia says, "I would say we are very proud of the work we are doing because we can see families staying together, in a better place. We're seeing parents that can fulfill their parental roles in a better way and children can feel they are loved. The kids who live in orphanages come from extreme poverty. They have parents but their parents are not able to support them due to financial reasons, or some of them have addictions or violence or family problems.

The newest program at the Hope Center is teaching the moms in the community how to make jewelry. It involves tediously crocheting high-quality silver into beautiful necklaces, earrings, bracelets, and brooches. The courses started in July 2013 and are taught by three girls who live in the Buckner transition home in Lima.

The girls in the transition home learned to make the jewelry in the spring of 2013 after a generous gift from WBGL, a radio station based in Champaign, Illinois. The gift made it possible for the girls to take classes so they could sell the jewelry. When Buckner decided to share the program in Pamplona, they thought having the girls teach the moms would be a great way for them to invest in the Buckner family.

MARY CRUZ ROMERO

Mary Cruz Romero, 23, was nervous when she first started teaching and was concerned that she would run out of patience. But it turns out she hasn't, and she said it's "very special" to be able to pass on the skill to other women. She went to the transition home in January 2011 after running away from home and her abusive father. She so badly wanted him to love her and when he didn't show her love, she internalized the stress. She used to have a lot of allergies from the stress, which caused acne and other skin issues. Mary Cruz was a challenge at first for Buckner staff, but Claudia said they would not give up on her.

Now, Mary Cruz finished school with a degree in international business. She has a steady job at a beauty product company where she helps with administrative tasks such as processing invoices, assisting with order requests and data entry. Without Buckner, she knows her life wouldn't be the same. Mary Cruz says "The first day, and until today, I always felt like it was a miracle because I couldn't believe I made it (into the Buckner transition home). At first, I was afraid but I have always been focused on my studies, and I still am. I have given all the best of myself, studying and developing as a person, and I really don't have enough words to simply say thanks. I hope I have always shown that appreciation, and I always will. They are a part of my life, the only family I have — forever."

Mary Cruz has gone through counseling, spiritual development, and a lot of personal growth during her stay at the girls transition home. When reflecting on Mary Cruz's experience, Claudia says "It's amazing how she's so much better from the inside that you can see it on the outside. Now she looks like a beautiful, healthier young girl. We are very proud of her."

MELBA MORAN

Talleres Artesanales is typically too far from the Hope Center for families to get to so Claudia leads Buckner Peru staff to them. They've helped several women to run a community dining room, Comedor Padre Arrupe, a cooperative effort where each family brings some food and cooks with each other, two meals a day. The kitchen was started by Melba Moran several years ago. At first, it was hard because the dilapidated structure made it easy for vandals to break in, but a mission team from Stephenville, Texas, constructed something more safe and secure.

Melba, now in her early 50s, grew up "extremely poor." She grew up hungry and she said she hates to see anyone suffer in the same way. They have meager equipment and limited supplies, but Moran is dedicated to the kitchen. In fact, she has slept there to keep watch. Buckner

Peru staff has helped her organize the kitchen and implement nutritional meals. The kitchen, also situated on a hill, is another ray of hope beaming out of the community.

Although the kitchen was operational, it was not in very good condition. Claudia saw that much improvement was needed, including improvement in space and sanitary conditions. Dogs were allowed to sleep in the kitchen, and Melba also slept there overnight. Claudia organized a mission group from the U.S. to come and expand the kitchen and she trained Melba to prepare meals and to keep the area sanitized and healthy. Now the kitchen has been expanded, sanitary conditions have improved and Melba is able to serve more people from the community due to the expansion.

URSULA ELENA PEREZ ASCONA

Ursula Elena Perez Ascona, 24, is one of the original four girls to enter into the Cuzco Girls Transitional Home. She wears a smile and a laugh that lights up all of Cuzco. It masks how afraid she is to leave the home. She's been there since 2008 and while she is scared, she's also ready — Buckner has prepared her well. Ursula says, "Buckner has been really significant in my life because without them, I wouldn't have finished a (college) career and I wouldn't be a professional. I wouldn't have a career at all. So they have been a huge part of my life all this time, and now that I'm leaving, I will miss them. I'm a bit afraid to live alone but I am very happy for the support."

Before she came to Buckner, Ursula lived at Buen Pastor, an all-girls orphanage, for five years. Her parents died when she was 14. Her brothers went to live somewhere else. Now, she goes back to Buen Pastor and volunteers her time to work with the girls. She said she is motivated to help others because of God and because of all the people who visited her when she lived there. She's working at a bank, Pro Mujer (Pro

Woman), which provides credit to small groups of women who have little economic resources. She said she loves her job and her dream is to move up through the company, and some day, have her own company. During her time in the home, she learned how to cook, crochet and how to take care of herself physically, emotionally, and spiritually. Without the home, Ursula guessed she'd probably have kids, and she definitely wouldn't have an education or a career.

Claudia has had direct participation with Ursula since her selection for the program. She has maintained a close relationship with her and has mentored her through this phase of her life. Ursula refers to Claudia as "mom." Claudia has taken the time to provide the kind of life coaching that Ursula needed to be successful and maintains that sense of family with her.

Ursula holds her Buckner experience close to her heart. She says, "Buckner helped me a lot in a spiritual way because it taught me what the Word of God is. Through this, I learned there are people out there who love us, despite not having my parents. Buckner has helped me develop as a person and improve my self-esteem because when my parents died, I wasn't that good, you know? I only thought about bad things, things that weren't right for my life, and Buckner has helped me go the right path in life."

LEADING BUCKNER PERU

Under Claudia's leadership, Buckner Peru has developed five programs that seek to intervene at different stages in the life cycle of children and families at risk. These programs include Family Hope Centers; Foster Care; Transitional Homes; Missions; and Humanitarian Aid.

Foster Care in Peru began under Claudia's leadership in 2007 through a signed agreement with the Ministry of Women and Social Development. Prior to the development of this program in Peru, a policy of de-institutionalization did not exist. All children in situations lacking appropriate protection were sent to shelters where in many cases they would remain until the age of 18. Claudia led her team to launch the first foster care program co-executed between the civil society and the State, an effort considered very difficult to accomplish in Peru. The Foster Care program sought to restore the rights of the children to live in a family whether in their own home or in a healthy family environment that provides the necessary protection and appropriate development without the deprivation of personal liberty. The program has been universally accepted. Leaders from other countries have sought out Claudia to lecture and train Buckner best practices in several South American countries.

Claudia defines her faith as intertwined with her work. Her faith anchors her conviction and the hope that things will improve as God guides her efforts. Claudia believes that God is a real God, a loving God, a God who cares about us, a God who really loves the little ones, and a God who is not limited to the forms that exist in our minds. She believes in the perfect plan of God in an imperfect world. She believes in a God that loves and cares for the ones who least can defend themselves; those who cannot vote; those who have no voice but want to be heard.

Claudia is a courageous leader working so that others might have a voice, especially for boys and girls. Claudia says that the children cannot vote during elections and often their care is not really important to politicians. She wants to be their voice and that's why she is interested in political advocacy for children. While her nature is to avoid conflict, she has been willing to face obstacles and has been willing to confront difficult situations. It takes courage to work toward social justice for those who have no voice.

Claudia said she once heard there are two important moments in life. The first is when we are born and the second when we discover why we are born. Claudia says she discovered why she was born in 2005. This is when she discovered that her life mission is to serve the less fortunate, to give voice to the disadvantaged, vulnerable ones and to defend their rights. This personal life mission provides a deep sense of passion never felt before. Claudia anchors her dream on Psalm 37:4: "Take delight in the Lord, and he will give you the desires of your heart." Her passion, sense of mission, and high moral vision for those she serves coupled with courageous leadership signals to me that Claudia has many victories for children in her future.

DISCUSSION QUESTIONS

1. In Joshua 1:9, we are encouraged to be courageous, to be strong. Why is this so important when serving vulnerable children and orphans in unjust situations?

2. Where do we find the courage to address injustice on behalf of others?

3. Why is fear and discouragement so prevalent when acting on behalf of those who have no voice, those who have suffered abuse, and those who have little hope?

4. What would the Lord lead you, your group, your church, your church network to do in response to the needs of the poorest families in your local community, children needing a family, or teen girls aging out of foster care?

5. After reading Claudia's story, how do you feel led to pray today?

6. Have you discovered why you were born? Have you discovered what God has set before your as your life mission?

ELEVEN:

Faith and Agents of Redemption

"And without faith it is impossible to please God, because anyone who comes to him must believe that he exists and that he rewards those who diligently seek him.

HEBREWS 11:6

The ministry of Buckner International is simply that, a ministry. And as such, the ministry of Buckner invites the ministry of agents of redemption from every corner of Christendom. Therefore, those who come to the table to serve with Buckner must come with faith. This ministry to the least of these, to visit orphans and widows, to shine hope into the lives of vulnerable children, orphans, and widows, is a faith proposition. Robert Cooke Buckner was a man of faith coupled with a habit of seeking the Kingdom first. The whole story of Buckner and the call of this book to mobilize the next generation of agents of redemption is built on the premise of faith described in Hebrews 11:6.

I am convinced that God delights in advancing our faith to the degree we depend on him, to the degree our faith is demonstrated in him to provide, to the degree that he will send the right people with the right gifts and abilities to us at just the right time. A casual view of Dr. Robert Cooke Buckner's life brings faith to the fore.

FAITH IN THE JOURNEY

Dr. Karen O'Dell Bullock, official Buckner historian, once said, "I think Robert Cooke Buckner perhaps would see Buckner International today with all of its vast programs and ministries across the globe and be very, very glad. I'm not so sure he would be surprised because he really was a man who believed that God was huge and God is able to do incredible things through people who were listening to him and believe in him. And I think Buckner would be very, very excited about the way that Buckner International today is ministering to so many different kinds of people in so many different kinds of ways."

Dr. Bullock, reflecting on the life and faith of Buckner, says that in the winter of 1859, just months before the Civil War would tear the nation apart, a 26-year-old Tennessee pastor would load his family onto a wagon and trek 900 miles to Texas, arriving in the spring of 1860. Stricken with typhoid pneumonia, Robert Cooke Buckner and his wife Vienna headed to the dry climate and Promised Land of Texas. He's called a band-box preacher by the time he becomes a preacher in Texas because he's so polished, not just in his attire — which was true — but his mind was active and fertile and his attitude toward people was open and embracing. Everyone noticed that he had these natural leadership abilities and they fell in love with him. In July 1860, Robert Cooke Buckner recieved a letter from the Paris, Texas church telling him: "We have already elected you to come be our pastor and would you also be with us for a revival service coming up?" So he went to Paris where he got to know the people there, loved that church, and he became their pastor.

Nearly 14 years later, in 1873, Buckner moved to Dallas. The village was little more than a trading post even as late as 1860, with a population of just 678. By the time Buckner arrived, the population had increased to more than 3,000. From Dallas, Buckner would start a statewide newspaper called *The Religious Messenger*. It was through the pages of his newspaper that Buckner would become a voice for needy children and the elderly. The Civil War had ended in 1865 and so many of the young men and the fathers of Texas had ridden away to war and some of them had died in the war; some of them had died because of wounds that they suffered when they came home. And so he himself, having recovered from typhoid pneumonia, knew how precarious life was, but his heart just broke because of all the hundreds of children that he saw either with one parent or with no parents; their families were often just scrambling to take in children that had been left orphaned. Buckner would often challenge leaders by saying "Brother Deacon, think about this for a moment. What if this was your child and you were gone. What would happen to your child? Think about this. Don't we need to do something? Think about it."

In July of 1877, Buckner summoned Baptist deacons from across the state to a meeting. The place would be his old home, First Baptist Church in Paris, Texas. After the preaching services, Buckner goes out and sits under this huge oak tree that's outside First Baptist Church Paris where everybody was waiting. Huge wagons in the yard, horses hitched up to the rails or turned out into the little pasture that was fenced nearby; lots of spreading oak trees there. So all the deacons that were in attendance went and sat in a big circle. Buckner sat down and they were talking and laughing and resting under that big oak tree. Then Buckner finally just pulled a dollar out of his pocket and laid it on his knee and said, "Just to get this thing started, here's the first dollar." Baylor University theology professor B.H. Carroll would give the second dollar. When the offering was taken, they had collected $27 to start Buckner Orphans Home. All of them knew that they were doing something important. All of them were acting out of their conviction that this was the right thing to do. With $27 secure, R.C. Buckner returned to Dallas, where he would launch a statewide campaign to raise $2,000 — the amount needed to open the orphans home. He was able to organize. He was a visionary. He was able to see what needed to be done, and he was able to convince people of the right thing to do. For Buckner, this was a journey of faith.

Buckner was quoted as saying, "It is more blessed to give than to receive. So it is more glorious to be a benefactor than a beneficiary. He is poor of spirit who is the beneficiary of all and the benefactor of none. Man's true glory consists in ministrations of goodness and benevolence to others." These kinds of sayings were rooted in the witness of Holy Scripture and an expression of his faith.

Buckner also said, "Money may be separated from religion, but religion can never be separated from money. There is but one kind of pure religion in the world and that is: To visit the fatherless and widows in their affliction, to keep himself unspotted from the world. Religion is piety and liberality — the heart given to God; the hand to man. What avails the offering of the lips when the light is withheld from the altar?"

From July 1877 until the charter was written in 1879, Buckner was writing articles, visiting, preaching in the pulpits of Texas Baptist churches all over the state, riding by horseback hundreds and hundreds of miles to meet people, to talk to people about his vision. On April 9th, 1879, the charter was officially filed with John D. Templeton, Secretary of the State of Texas in Austin. On December 2nd, eight months later, Buckner Orphans Home welcomed its first three orphan children — John and Alice Cruse from McKinney and John Jones from

Ellis County, whose parents had died in a woodchopper's camp on the Trinity River bottom. Buckner, an agent of redemption himself, lived and worked by faith, the kind of faith that depended on God for results. The people of Texas rallied to the call and cause. They embraced the movement — from the Gulf Coast to the Panhandle; from central Texas to the north. From little towns and hamlets; from villages and blossoming cities, they packed and shipped boxes of dry good, donated cows, boars and sows, turkey eggs and lumber. They sent their pennies, stitched quilts, canned jars of vegetables and they raised wheat for Father Buckner's children.

FAITH IN THE FAMILY

Dr. Robert Cooke Buckner lived a life of faith and works. He had a God-sized vision that depended on the response and cooperation of people compelled by their faith to take action all across Texas. Father Buckner handed out postcards with his picture on the front and on the back it said, "If any of you need help at any time, give this postcard to the nearest railway agent and that agent will help you come to see me and we will help you." One year, Buckner led a series of revivals at a church and soon after that, a whole family of children, seven of them, were orphaned. The oldest daughter's name was Kate. She was about 10 years old and she had six siblings. In the middle of the night, Kate got up, took the postcard and she went to every other house where her siblings were and she gathered up all her sisters and brothers, and in the early daylight hours she presented that postcard, with all of her brothers and sisters gathered around her, to the railway agent who helped them get to Dallas. And she walked up to the gate at Dallas and she handed the postcard to the first person she saw and said, "Is it really true that Father Buckner will help me? Because we need a home." The children were welcomed and found a new home and a new family at Buckner.

The ministry of Buckner has always been characterized by faith. The kind of faith that pleases God, the kind of faith that depends on God to move his people, the kind of faith that causes friends to become donors, the kind of faith that draws God's people into the story of redemption, especially for the least of these. This kind of faith is an expression of Ephesians 3:20: "Now to him who is able to do immeasurably more than all we ask or imagine, according to his power that is at work within us, to him be glory in the church and in Christ Jesus throughout all generations, for ever and ever! Amen." It is my desire to ask and imagine a Buckner that serves vulnerable children, orphans, and seniors according to God's power at work within us. It is my hope to lead Buckner by faith the same way Dr. Robert Cooke Buckner did. Today I am making the appeal for agents of redemption to rise up from congregations, life groups, Bible study groups, Bible colleges, seminaries, and university campuses all over the planet to engage the world with us by shining the hope of Christ into the lives of "the least of these." Without this kind of faith, it is impossible to please God. But with this kind of faith, we can fulfill God's purpose and live up to the legacy we received from our founder. Will you join us in this mission? Will you join us in this faith journey?

DISCUSSION QUESTIONS

1. In Hebrews 11:6, the writer suggests that we cannot please God apart from faith. Why is faith so critical when attempting to do great things for the Kingdom of God?

2. In Ephesians 3:20, Paul suggests that God is able to do far more than we ask or imagine. What do you imagine for the future of vulnerable children and orphans around the world?

3. Throughout history, ordinary people with vision, like Dr. Buckner, accomplished extraordinary things for God. What is your vision for bringing the Kingdom of God very near to vulnerable children and orphans?

4. What would the Lord lead you, your group, your church, your church network to do in response to the needs of vulnerable children and orphans around the world?

5. What might you attempt to do for vulnerable children and orphans that would cause you to stretch or grow your faith?

Conclusion

"Let the redeemed of the Lord tell their story — those he redeemed from the hand of the foe, those he gathered from the lands, from east and west, from north and south."

PSALM 107:2-3

I have attempted to tell my story of redemption and invite you to join the redeemer of history in his activity among the least of these, the vulnerable child, the orphan, and the widow. For all the days the Lord allows me to live, I plan to pursue this vision of God's heart to take what was intended for harm and turn it into good for the poorest of the poor, for many of the 151 million orphans and vulnerable children in the world today, for the least of these in our global village, to the forgotten, the abused, the abandoned, and neglected children in our world. For over 135 years, the ministry of Buckner has sought to do this work by serving the least of these among us.

In this volume, I outlined what I mean by redemption as rescue, as a transition to the Kingdom of Jesus, and as the forgiveness of our sins. I traced the concept of redemption through the Old Testament and the New Testament and then outlined a definition of an agent of redemption. Simply stated, it is a person driven by compassion, conviction, and courage to shine hope into the lives of vulnerable children and orphans. I have attempted to demonstrate how redemptive work is done in the global village and in the local village. I raised a challenge for Christian organizations to collaborate for the benefit of others. Agents of redemption like Dickson Masindano, Cynthia Rentie, and Claudia Leon set the bar very high for all of us. And finally, I have pointed out that the work of agents of redemption and the challenge to engage and mobilize Jesus followers in this movement requires faith if we are going to please God in our lifetime for his Kingdom.

I imagine and ask for a Buckner that provides permanency for children in families. I strongly believe that the best place for a child to grow and thrive is within the context of a loving and healthy family environment. I am talking about families grounded in biblical faith, families that have deep spiritual roots after the Jesus way. What I have in mind are families that believe their children have a purpose in redemptive history. I am thinking of families that love and nurture their children to become all God has intended them to be. Many children may have an opportunity for a family through inter-country adoption. However, most will not have the option to leave their country of origin. I wonder what difference we might make in the life of one of the least of these. I am inviting you to help us find families for them in their country, city, community, and culture. We can move children to permanent and healthy family environments if we work together. We can shine hope into the life of a child by offering the gift of family through foster care and adoption.

I imagine and ask for a Buckner that provides family preservation. There are so many families in the world that struggle to survive every day. Frankly, this breaks my heart. They do the best they can with what they have and what they have come to know. This was the life experience of my family only two generations ago. Deep in my heart is the memory of those who came before us, struggling to survive, hoping for a better life. Those of us that live in places of relative affluence have a responsibility to develop healthy and strong families in our global village. Healthy and prospering families are the bedrock of any society and culture. J-shaped families provide wholesome and healthy environments grounded by the principles of Christian scripture for raising children. We can shine hope brightly into the lives of struggling families by providing a hand-up rather than merely a hand-out. We are making a difference in communities all over the planet but we could do more with your help.

I am totally convinced that the best way to make a better person is with Jesus. As we pursue child permanency and family preservation, we also point those we serve to Jesus as our exemplary mentor for life. Our primary way of pointing to Jesus is in the way we serve. However, we are always ready to provide an answer for the hope within us. When you engage with us, you become an agent of redemption. I invite you to tell your story of redemption and join us in our effort to turn what was intended for harm into good. I invite you to give of yourself in order to directly transform the lives of vulnerable children and orphans. You may want to consider the gift of your story, your time, the gift of your talent, the gift of your treasure, or the gift of family.

THE GIFT OF YOUR REDEMPTION STORY

Every person who has come to faith in Jesus has a story to tell. Before Jesus found you, you were an orphan, held in the space of dominion for evil. You were alone in a depraved world with no one to care for you. But then, you came to faith in Jesus and everything changed. When you realize how much you have been forgiven; when you consider the grace of God and the love he has shown you through the gift of his own son; when you reflect on the great sacrifice Jesus made on the cross to forgive you, to redeem you, to show God's love for you, would you not, in turn, have much to give? Whoever is forgiven much, loves much. This is your story of redemption. Look at Psalm 139:13-16 and consider how God created you for a purpose. Consider how he knew all your days before you took one breath. Look at Jeremiah 33:1-3 and consider asking the Lord to show you how he wants to use you. Consider Jeremiah 29:11 and consider the plans the Lord has for you.

The best place to start is reconstructing your redemption story. Such a salvation calls for a response. We are saved to serve; redeemed for a purpose; and bought with a price. We do not belong to ourselves and must not live to ourselves. We belong to the wider and broader story of redemption so tell your story. How does your story begin? You may have to go back a generation. When did the gospel first come to your family? Where did your family first hear about Jesus? Who brought the good news to you? How did the story of God's love come to you, through your family? What were the things that were intended to harm you? How did God reverse those events and turn them into good? What is the reason for your life? What is the purpose of your life? How is God taking what was intended to harm you and turning it now into good, even the redemption of others? How is the gospel going through you? How is God's story of redemption activating all the gifts, abilities, potential, and plans for the Kingdom through your life? How are you becoming an agent of redemption? How are you becoming the hands and feet of Jesus? But don't stop with your story. Consider how to give of your time, your talent, and your treasure.

THE GIFT OF TIME

Volunteers, university, college, and graduate students, and professionals have time they might consider contributing in collaboration with Buckner to serve the least of these. You might consider contributing your time in collaboration with Buckner ministry among children and their families. Every year, about 6,000 short-term volunteers travel with Buckner to the Rio Grande Valley and to seven countries around the world to give of their time to serve children and families. Volunteers also travel to Buckner campuses and ministry sites in Texas on a weekly basis to provide support to foster group families and clients. You might consider volunteering as a mentor, a tutor, or an encourager among children who need support in Foster Group Care homes, at a Family Place program or at Family Hope Centers. If you are a student, you might have the luxury of international travel through Project Go to spend your time in the global south with children struggling for a better life. If you are not able to travel internationally, you may give of your time domestically in the Rio Grande Valley or in Dallas at our Humanitarian Aid Center. The gift of your time in God's economy is priceless and deeply meaningful to the children and families you will meet. Visit www.itsyourmission.com to learn more about ways you might give of your time to shine hope into the lives of vulnerable children and their families.

THE GIFT OF TALENT

God has blessed you with incredible talent that can be used to bless other children and their families. You might consider collaborating with Buckner through your profession. The profession you have been called to do carries with it skills from the workplace that can be used to serve vulnerable children and their families. You might be a teacher, an ESL instructor, a business leader or CEO, a medical professional, a construction professional, an architect, an artist, a musician, a librarian, a government leader, a professor, an engineer, a science professional or any number of professions with skills that can benefit the least of these. You can deploy these talents in local and international mission projects that will make a big difference as an agent of redemption. Visit www.itsyourmission.com and learn more about ways you might give of your time to shine hope into the lives of vulnerable children and their families.

THE GIFT OF TREASURE

The third gift you can bring to the table is the gift of your treasure. When you give of your financial resources, you collaborate with Buckner to make the provision of services possible to the poorest of the poor, the least of these around the world. No gift is too small to touch a life of a child here in the United States and around the world. Even the gift of a pair of shoes can make a difference in a child's life. In some countries, a pair of shoes might even save a child's life. A brand new pair of shoes can prevent parasites in contaminated water from entering a child's blood-stream at the point of an abrasion from a sharp object. Shoes can be given through the Buckner Shoes for Orphan Souls program.

Since 2000 Buckner has collected and distributed over 3 million pairs of shoes to children and their families in over 85 countries around the world. Over the last 15 years, we have seen churches, civic groups like Rotarians, schools, radio listeners, businesses, and government agencies participate in shoe drives as community service projects. Each year over 6,000 volunteers visit the Humanitarian Aid Warehouse in Dallas to sort shoes and prepare them for shipment. Few experiences are more powerful and life transforming than to kneel before a child to remove old shoes and socks, wash and dry their feet and place new socks and shoes on them. Visit www.shoesfororphansouls.com to learn more about engaging this project to share from your treasure.

You may want to also consider making a financial gift to Buckner to serve vulnerable children where it is most needed. We raise financial support for domestic programs to subsidize state support and we raise 100 percent of all financial resources used in international work annually as our only source of support. One hundred cents on the dollar raised by our development team goes to programs supporting children and their families. The overhead cost for development is covered from another source. We receive gifts from individuals, foundations, churches, and civic groups every year to support all of our programs. Visit www.buckner.org for more information about sharing from your treasure. You may want to learn more about our ministry through my blog at www.bucknerprez.com and plug into ways God can use you as an agent of redemption.

THE GIFT OF FAMILY

Perhaps one of the most meaningful and lasting impacts you can make is to be a family for a child looking for a place to call home through foster care or adoption. Foster care may last a few weeks to a few months. Adoption, though, is forever. We feature Foster-to-Adopt programs where a child may begin in foster care and then transition to adoption with his or her foster family. We have several programs that may be of interest to you if you are led to participate this way. See www.beafamily.org for more information.

Join us! Join our movement to shine hope on the lives of vulnerable children and orphans. Tell your story of redemption through Buckner ministry. Find your role in God's redemptive work in history. Your life will never be the same.

DISCUSSION QUESTIONS

1. In Psalm 107:2-3, the Psalmist David, suggests the redeemed person should tell his or her story. What is your story of redemption?

2. How does your story of redemption connect with God's redemptive work in history?

3. God has created each one of us for a purpose and with a design to serve him. How would you envision serving through Buckner to reach out to the least of these?

4. What would the Lord lead you, your group, your church, your church network to do in response to the needs of vulnerable children and orphans around the world?

5. What might you attempt to do for vulnerable children and orphans that would be an expression of your story of redemption?

ACKNOWLEDGEMENTS

I dedicated this book to the leaders and staff at Buckner International and affiliated Buckner NGO staff who so faithfully serve every day as agents of redemption. Thank you for offering your talents each day across the world to work toward redemptive transformation in the lives of those we serve. I am honored to serve with an outstanding team of senior leaders such as David Slover, Tony Lintelman, Steve Wakefield, Charlie Wilson, JoAnn Cole, and Henry Jackson. You led the way for our team and ministry while I was away from the office writing this book. I want to thank my office support team of Gilbert Montez, Cheryl Jones, and Glynnis Barrett for their assistance during the months I juggled priorities to write this book. Special thanks to Scott Collins for guiding this project and for his team of writers including Russ Dilday, Whitney Farr, Lauren Sturdy, and Chelsea White, who "tell the Buckner story by telling Buckner stories" of those we serve. One of the reasons why Buckner International has a 136-year history and legacy is the excellent governance leaders on the Buckner board. This book could not have been written without the encouragement and vision of the Buckner International Board of Trustees who wisely guide this ministry. Thank you for your Christ-like spirit, your wisdom, and your belief in me as I lead Buckner. Thanks to the many staff, pastors, volunteers, donors, friends, and clients of Buckner for allowing me to include your story. You are the inspiration behind the idea for this book.

Finally, I wish to thank Belinda, my wife and ministry partner of over 33 years, for her support, prayers, patience, and encouragement. Your words of encouragement at just the right time refueled my energy and encouraged me to keep writing until I finished. Thanks also to Joshua, David, and Thomas, our three sons, for your encouragement along the way, for walking this journey with me, and for recognizing the Lord's redemptive presence in your life. I love you more than you may ever know. I thank the Lord Jesus for his love for me, for saving me, for calling me to serve him, and for taking what was intended to harm me and turning it into good over and over again, for his name, his will, and his Kingdom.

NOTES:

INTRODUCTION

1. For a complete study of the transformation of BUA see Reyes, A. L. (2009). Intercultural relationships in organizational transformation: A single case-study of Baptist University of the Américas. A Dissertation for the PhD in Global Leadership at Andrews University, Berrien Springs, Michigan.

2. For an exploration of educational opportunities for under-represented students in higher education see Reyes, A. L. (2006). *Can Baptist institutions of higher education meet the needs of increasingly diverse constituencies?* In Schmeltekopf, D. D. & Vitanza, D. M, The future of Baptist higher education. Waco, Texas: Baylor University Press.

3. For a broader story on the in-grafting of my family into the Texas Baptist family see Reyes, A. L. (2005). *Unification to Integration: A brief history of the Hispanic Baptist Convention of Texas* in Baptist History and Heritage: The Baptist Community, Vol. XL, Winter 2005, No. 1. Brentwood, TN: Baptist History and Heritage Society.

4. Ibid, 48.

5. For a broader account of my personal narrative, see Reyes, A. L. (2010). *Puentes: Journey notes of a bridge person*, The Journal of Applied Christian Leadership., Vo. 4, No. 1, spring 2010. Berrien Springs, MI: Christian Leadership Center, Andrews University.

ONE:

1. This imagery is from A.T. Robertson's Word Pictures in the New Testament: Volume IV, The Epistles of Paul (Nashville: Broadman Press, 1931) 477.

2. Hans Conzelmann, σκότος in Theological dictionary of the New Testament, Gerhard Kittel & Gerhard Friedrich, eds. (Grand Rapids: W. B. Eerdmans Publishing Company, 1971) 423-445.

3. Alfred Barry, *The Epistles to the Ephesians, Philippians, and Colossians*, in Ellicott's Commentary on the Whole Bible: A verse by verse explanation, Charles John Ellicott, ed., vol. 8, (Grand Rapids, MI: Zondervan Publishing House, nd) 99.

4. William F. Arndt and F. Wilbur Gingrich, A Greek-English Lexicon of the New Testament and other Early Christian Literature, 2nd ed., (Chicago, IL: The University of Chicago Press, 1979). 499.

5. Alfred Barry, 99.

6. Arthur F. Glasser, Announcing the Kingdom: The Story of God's Mission in the Bible (Grand Rapids, MI: Baker Academic, 2003) 190-198.

7. Tullian Tchividjian, Unfashionable: Making a difference in the world by being different. (Colorado Springs, Colorado: Multnomah Books, 2009) 70.

8. W. E. Vine, Vine's Expository Dictionary of New Testament Words (Westwood, New Jersey: Barbour and Company, Inc., 1952), 264.

9. This imagery is from A. T. Robertson, Word Pictures in the New Testament: Volume IV, The Epistles of Paul (Nashville: Broadman Press, 1931) 347.

TWO:

1. Leslie C. Allen, Word Biblical Commentary: Psalm 101-150, David Hubbard, Glenn Barker, & John Watts, eds. (Waco, Texas: Word Books Publisher, 1983) 191-196.

2. Harrelson, W. (1964). Interpreting the Old Testament (New York: Holt, Rinehart, and Winston, Inc.). 439.

3. LaSor, W., Hubbard, D. & Bush, F. (1982). Old Testament Survey: The message, form, and background of the Old Testamant (Grand Rapids, MI: William B. Eerdmans Publishing Company), 616.

THREE

1. Cranfill, J. & Walker J. (1996). *R.C. Buckner's Life of Faith and Works: Comprising the Story of the Career of the Preacher, Editor, Presiding Officer, Philanthropist, and Founder of Buckner Orphans Home*. (Austin, Texas: Nortex Press), 104.

2. Harrison, E. F. (1984). Redeemer, Redemption in *Evangelical Dictionary of Theology*, Walter A. Elwell, editor (Grand Rapids: Baker Book House).

3. Webber, O. (1981). *Foundations of dogmatics*, Vol. I (Grand Rapids, MI: William B. Eerdmans Publishing Company.

4. Vines, W. E. (1940). *Vine's expository dictionary of New Testament words*, (Westwood, NJ: Barbour and Company Inc.).

5. See Galatians 3:13, 4:5, Ephesians 5:16, Colossians 4:5, and Revelation 5:9, 14:3 & 4.

6. For Lutrosis, see Luke 24:21, Titus 2:14, 1 Peter 1:18, Luke 1:68, 2:38, Hebrews 9:12,

and for Apolutrosis (stronger form of releasing) see Hebrews 11:35, Luke 21:28, 2 Thessalonians 2:8, Romans 3:24, Ephesians 1:7, Colossians 1:14, Romans 6:4, Hebrews 9:15, Romans 8:23, 1 Corinthians 1:30, Ephesians 1:14 and 4:30.

7. Buchsel, F. (1964). Agorazo, Exagorazo in *Theological Dictionary of the New Testament*, Charles Kittel (ed), Vol. 1, (Grand Rapids: Wm. B. Eerdmans Publishing Company.

8. Buchsel, F. (1964). Luo in *Theological Dictionary of the New Testament*, Charles Kittel (ed), Vol. 4, (Grand Rapids: Wm. B. Eerdmans Publishing Company.

9. Vincent, D. (1946). *Word Studies in the New Testament*, Vol. 1, (Grand Rapids, MI: Wm. B. Eerdmans Publishing Company.

FOUR

1. Romans 12:2

2. 1 Corinthians 2:16

3. Wolf, T. A., (2010). Lifecode: An examination of the shape, the nature, and the usage of the oikoscode, a replicative nonformal learning pattern of ethical education for leaders and community groups. A dissertation for the doctor of philosophy degree at Andrews University. Berrien Springs, Michigan: Andrews University.

4. Ibid, 133.

5. Ibid, 133

6. Micah 6:8

7. Mathew 23:23

8. 1 Corinthians 13:13

9. Wolf, 130.

10. Ibid, 127.

11. Ibid, 216.

12. Cranfill J. B. & Walker, J. L. (1915). *R.C. Buckner's Life of Faith and Works: Comprising the Story of the Career of the Preacher, Editor, Presiding Officer, Philanthropist, and Founder of Buckner Orphan's Home.* Dallas, Texas: Buckner Orphan's Home.

13. Ibid, 41.

14. Ibid, 64-65.

15. Ibid, 75-76.

16. These comments are from a paper delivered by Karen O. Bullock, PhD entitled "Whispers from the Depths: Buckner and the Secrets About Sea Changes," on September 10, 2013 at the Annual Buckner Leadership Retreat at Camp Buckner.

17. Ibid.

18. Ibid.

19. Ibid.

20. Ibid.

21. Bullock, K.O. (1991). *The Life and Contributions of Robert Cooke Buckner: Progenitor of Organized Social Christianity among Texas Baptists, 1860-1919*. A doctoral dissertation at Southwestern Baptist Theological Seminary, Fort Worth, Texas.

22. Ibid.

23. Ibid, 10.

24. Ibid, 10.

25. Ibid, 10, 16.

26. James 2:26b, NIV

27. Bullock, Whispers from the Depths.

28. Ibid.

29. Thom Wolf, WV3: Worldvoice, Worldview, and Worldvenue - the voice, view, and venue lifezones of the planet, 16-26 in Thom Wolf, *Social Change and Development: A Research Template*. New Delhi: University Institute 2013

30. Ibid. 18

31. Ibid, 20.

32. Ibid, 21.

FIVE

1. Cranfill J. B. & Walker, J. L., 86-88.

2. Bullock, The Life and Contributions of Robert Cooke Buckner, 16

3. Ibid, 109.

4. Ibid, 124.

SIX

1. Jenkins, P. (2013). "Christianity's Global Past and Christianity's Global Future" a lecture delivered to the Annual Pastor's Conference at Camp Buckner Hill Country Retreat, October 29, 2013. For additional information see Jenkins, P. (2002 & 2006). The next Christendom: The rise of global christianity & The new faces of christianity: Believing the bible in the global south.

2. Krogstad, J. M., Gonzalez-Barrera, A. & Lopez, M. H. "Children 12 and under are fastest growing group of unaccompanied minors at US border. Pew Research Center, July 22, 2014, accessed at http://www.pewresearch.org/fact-tank/2014/07/22/children-12-and-under-are-fastest-growing-group-of-unaccompanied-minors-at-u-s-border/ on February 20, 2015.

NOTES

SEVEN

1. Wolf, T. (2010).
2. Wolf, T. (2013).

ABOUT THE AUTHOR:

Albert L. Reyes, a native of Corpus Christi, Texas, was raised in Rialto, California and South Texas. An experienced business leader in telecommunications, pastoral leader, and university president, he serves as the sixth President and CEO of Buckner International, a global Christian ministry founded in 1879 in Dallas, Texas focused on serving vulnerable children, orphans, seniors, and their families. His travels have taken him across the USA and to over 17 countries, primarily in the global south, where he has engaged heads of state, senior level government leaders, faith community leaders, leaders of non-government organizations, volunteers, donors, and marketplace leaders to shine hope into the lives of children and families in some of the poorest communities on the planet. He earned a bachelor of business administration degree in management from Angelo State University, a master's of divinity degree and doctor of ministry degree in missiology from Southwestern Seminary, and a doctor of philosophy degree in global leadership from Andrews University. He has been a guest lecturer on leadership, leading social change, and organizational transformation at universities in the USA and abroad including Harvard University, Dallas Baptist University, Hardin Simmons University, Angelo State University, and the Pontifical Catholic University of Peru in Lima. He and his wife, Dr. Belinda A. Reyes, live in Dallas and they have three adult sons.